U0872648

新视角英语文学与文化系列教材

丛书主编　刘　岩

广告文化选读

丁少彦　　编

武汉大学出版社

图书在版编目(CIP)数据

广告文化选读/丁少彦编. —武汉:武汉大学出版社,2011.9
(新视角英语文学与文化系列教材/刘岩丛书主编)
ISBN 978-7-307-09163-4

Ⅰ.广… Ⅱ.丁… Ⅲ.①英语—高等学校—教材 ②广告文化—西方国家 Ⅳ.H319.4:F

中国版本图书馆 CIP 数据核字(2011)第 182891 号

责任编辑:谢群英 责任校对:刘 欣 版式设计:支 笛

出版发行:武汉大学出版社 (430072 武昌 珞珈山)
(电子邮件:cbs22@whu.edu.cn 网址:www.wdp.com.cn)
印刷:湖北省荆州市今印印务有限公司
开本:880×1230 1/32 印张:7.625 字数:208 千字
版次:2011 年 9 月第 1 版 2011 年 9 月第 1 次印刷
ISBN 978-7-307-09163-4/H·612 定价:18.00 元

版权所有,不得翻印;凡购买我社的图书,如有缺页、倒页、脱页等质量问题,请与当地图书销售部门联系调换。

总　序

我们所处的时代是一个多元共生的时代。国际政治的多极化走向、经济的全球化趋势、社会的信息化局面以及文化的多元化态势正快速改变着我们的生活。科学技术的高速发展以及新兴学科的不断涌现加剧了世界各国文化的交流、碰撞和合作。如何培养适应新时代发展和需要的人才，这是我们这一代教育工作者面临的新课题和新挑战。

高等学校外语专业教学指导委员会英语组于 2000 年 3 月修订的《高等学校英语专业英语教学大纲》明确规定了高等学校英语专业的培养目标："高等学校英语专业培养具有扎实的英语语言基础和广博的文化知识并能熟练地运用英语在外事、教育、经贸、文化、科技、军事等部门从事翻译、教学、管理、研究等工作的复合型英语人才。"这样的描述为我们编写英语专业教材和组织英语专业教学提供了重要依据。我校在长期的外语教学和研究实践中践行"明德尚行，学贯中西"的校训，着力推进外语与专业的融合，致力于培养一专多能、"双高"（思想素质高、专业水平高）、"两强"（外语实践能力强、信息技术运用能力强）、具有国际视野和创新意识的国际通用型人才。这要求全面提高学生的综合素质，包括拓宽人文学科知识，加强人文素质，培养创新精神，提高独立分析问题和解决问题的能力。

正是在这样的环境和背景下，我院精心策划并组织骨干教师编写了这套《新视角英语文学与文化系列教材》。这套教材可以用于英语专业高年级文学、文化、翻译等专业课和选修课的教学，也可化，全球化语境下的文化特点和跨国广告特征；第六部分介绍工业化社会和科技之上的思想意识对自然环境的破坏，生态女性主义文化思潮和广告对环保意识的商业化挪用。为了帮助学生理解文章旨意，在每篇文章后附加了思考题，供学生理解、讨论之用。

本教材所选取的相关文献，主要出版时间为20世纪末和21世纪初，所选范围主要来自英美学者有关论题的经典著作和报刊文献，出处均详列于每篇选文之后。对于原作者及其相关出版社，编者在此表示衷心的感谢。

本教材受到广东外语外贸大学211工程办公室和香港大学美国文化研究中心的鼎力协助，在此表示衷心的感谢。

囿于编者水平和编写时间，其中难免有不妥、疏漏之处。恳请各位专家与学者不吝赐教，以便编者再版时予以纠正。

编　者

2011年7月于广州白云

前　言

广告随着西方工业化的发展和殖民扩张的进程而产生，并随着营销和消费的需要而成为当代生活中重要的文化形式。广告充满了广播、报纸、杂志、电视、网络等空间，生产着生活方式和价值观念。在形式上，广告是20世纪最有代表性的艺术形式（詹姆森语）。因此，解读广告的文化符号成了当代人媒体文化认知的重要部分。国(境)外(美国、加拿大、中国香港等)的高等学校自20世纪90年代以来已相继设置广告文化研究课程，研究和分析广告中的视觉符号与人类社会、文化、消费、环境，以及全球—本土化进程的关系。因此作为外语学院的文化与传媒教育，引入广告文化课程，编写广告文化教材，帮助学生认知广告文化是很有必要的。

在编写本教材的过程中，笔者尝试从培养学生的文化认知和文化分析能力的视角出发，同时兼顾学生的外语语言能力的提高，尽可能地让学生精读原著，把握原著的旨意。因此节选了一些西方广告文化研究材料，供学生阅读、思考，并为教学进行主题分析和讨论之用。

本书从文化研究角度出发编写材料，围绕性别身份、种族再现、青年文化时尚、消费与全球广告、广告绿色营销等专题组织内容。具体地说，本书由六个专题部分组成：第一部分介绍广告的历史和定义及常用广告研究方法；第二部分批评广告中的身体再现及变化中的广告身体形象；第三部分批评美国广告对黑人族裔和美国以外的文化的他者化再现；第四部分介绍时尚、品牌的文化意义，及青年品牌时尚的文化精神；第五部分内容为消费社会和多元文以为其他专业的学生提供必要的相关专业知识。我们期待这套教材能够以培养学生人文素质为根本原则，以加强学生人文修养、增强学生创新能力为目标，帮助学生批判地吸收世界文化精髓并弘扬中国优秀文化传统。

这套教材的策划和出版得到武汉大学出版社的积极推动和热情支持，没有他们的努力就不会有这套教材的问世。我院教师把多年教学经验积淀成书，每一本教材都凝结着他们的智慧和心血。还有我院一批渴求知识的学生，是他们的勤学好问让我们看到了工作的价值，也正是在教学相长的过程中我们的教材得到了不断的完善。在这套教材即将面世之际，让我们对所有参与教材编写和出版的人士表示衷心的感谢和敬意！也请同行专家对教材的缺憾不吝赐教。

广东外语外贸大学英语语言文化学院　刘岩博士

目　录

Chapter 1 Understanding Advertising

Introduction

Althoug hadvertising is nowadays familiar to everyone in daily life as an important medium of popular culture, it is difficult to give advertising a simple, clear-cut, privileged definition, as advertising is multi-faceted and saturated with subtle complexity. Thus, to understand advertising, firstly, we have to start from its very beginning — to capture a historical/dynamic perspective in order to understand the changing images and roles of advertising in relation to the economic, socio-cultural and technological development. Specifically, a brief history of American advertising is introduced to present such a perspective, as advertising has been fast developed in the last one hundred years and American advertising has been most influential during this period. Then, major approaches of advertising are introduced to give a relatively more comprehensive view of the dimensions and the inflections of advertising.

As methodology is important in study advertising, the second part of this chapter concerns the introduction to two approaches of advertising: semiotic analysis and content analysis. Roland Barthes' pondering on the mythic language of advertising is introduced to present the way of semiotic analysis and the relation between advertising and cultural representation. Besides, a content analysis is introduced so that a quantitative analysis can be used to measure the message of a large number of ads. In fact, the combination of the two methods can ensure a more reliable analysis of advertising, especially when an archive of advertisements is concerned.

Part I Understanding Advertising

Passage 1

History of Advertising in the United States

This history of advertising technique chronicles the movement from face-to-face selling messages to the stilted, repetitive, printed advertisements of early newspapers to the dynamism of mass communication by radio and television to the re-personalization of messages via cable, Internet, and direct mail. It is a story of sellers struggling to find the best means to attract buyers. [...]

1. European Precedents

(In the 1600s, an age of exploration and discovery), [...] (European) settlers would decide to leave home and strike out for a new life abroad. [...] Advertising played its role in fueling these dreams and aspirations. To promote colonial ventures, sponsors placed ads in British newspapers: ads that promised solutions to nagging problems, ads that offered the fulfillment of dreams and the realization of hopes.

In addition to this outward expansion, the world came to England as well. Strange, unusual, and wonderful things were brought from far-away ports: spices from India, carpets from Persia, tobacco and tomatoes from the New World, porcelain from China, and coffee from Arabia. Each of these commodities had to be introduced to the consuming public and integrated into their lives — and advertising was one of the means of doing so.

2. Colonial America

Ships brought English goods and African slaves to colonial America and took raw materials (cotton, sugar, and tobacco) home on the return trip. These raw materials were in turn processed and either used in England or re-exported. Early settlers in the American colonies produced most of what they consumed at home, but a few precious goods were bought in stores. Newspapers were scarce — the first in America were published around 1700 — and the ads they carried were few, often reappearing from issue to issue, and tended to carry messages in the form "Just Imported — A Variety of Goods". These ads contained few illustrations and seldom mentioned price. [...]

A key figure in colonial American advertising was none other than Benjamin Franklin. As publisher of *The Philadelphia Gazette* and *Poor Richard's Almanac*, he changed advertising style by including simple illustrations to accompany the words in ads. He began also to provide more details about benefits and uses than many of the ads that preceded him.

3. The Age of the Newspaper

James Gordon Bennett, publisher of the *New York Herald* from 1835 to 1867, is one of the most flamboyant characters in the history of American mass media. [...] He latched onto the idea of raising the cost of advertisements to lower the cost of newspapers, a practice that continues into the present. He put an end to the seemingly endless repetition of ads from issue to issue that had characterized American newspapers from the colonial period well into the 19th century.

Bennett first limited an ad's run to two weeks, and then later to a single day, giving readers cause to read ads more carefully. He also began printing ads throughout his paper, even on the front page, thus treating ads like news. To ensure readers and thus sales of his newspaper, Bennett did not shy away from the sensational — in either news or ads. He broke with the typical focus of other editors on political news and included stories from police files, courts, sports, theatres, and other events that had mass appeal.

4. Travelling Salesman in the Small Towns

Meanwhile, direct selling messages remained common in smaller towns all over America. Store clerks continued to deal face-to-face with their customers, discussing the uses and benefits for the products they sold. However, by the mid-1800s itinerant salesmen had also become a part of American commerce. [...]

Salesmanship [...] differs from advertising in its use of face-to-face rather than mass-mediated communications and selling techniques. The promotional and selling methods of salesmen are the important elements in the history of advertising. Whether to a merchant, an assembled crowd, or just a single customer, a salesman displayed his merchandise and adjusted his pitch to the needs and interests of his audience.

5. Advertising Agents

As America recovered from the Civil War (1861 — 1865), commerce and newspapers once again took their place in the fabric of society. In the 1860s and 1870s, the forerunners of modern advertising agents came on the scene. First offering to physically take ads from the shops of busy tradesmen to the offices of newspaper publishers, ad men provided a service that business found desirable. Two of the earliest agencies were N. W. Ayer in Philadelphia and J. Walter Thompson in New York. These agencies collected circulation figures of newspapers and magazines and based their commissions on readership.

It was a short step from media placement to another service that indeed marked the beginnings of modern advertising. The agents offered to write the copy that would be placed in newspapers. By the turn of the 20th century, several advertising agencies had set up business in cities across America, marking the beginnings of a shift away from direct sales techniques to mass-communicated advertising.

The consequence of this difference (from the salesmanship) is a shift from individually tailored messages, to those that must be relevant to a broad and diverse audience. Both the unregulated sales tactics and advertising claims of the 19th century engendered watchful suspicion on the part of consumers, making many people wary of the actual truth in the communications. Both salesmen and advertisers work as intermediaries between sellers and buyers — a role not much appreciated in American society where dislike of all sorts of intermediaries (advertisers, lawyers, brokers, and agents) is frequently a part of the culture. A final important point of comparison is that both salesman and advertisers must attempt to understand the consumer's viewpoints, needs, and wants in order to do their jobs well.

6. Billboards, Trade Cards, and Other Advertising Strategies

In the late 19th and early 20th centuries, advertising agencies came into their own by offering a wide range of services to the clients who hired them to help promote goods and services. One advertising gimmick was the inclusion of trade cards in packages of cigarettes and other forms of tobacco. Consumers were encouraged to collect entire series of glamorous women, movie stars, Indian chiefs, wonders of the world, and so on. Another technique invented by advertising agents was prizes in return for a specified number of proofs of purchase.

By the end of the 19th century, advertising had proliferated beyond the newspaper and magazine to posters and billboards in public spaces. Trains and streetcars typically carried such notices and the public streets and byways were filled with billboards and other advertising posters.

All such techniques [...] were ways in which advertising agents expanded their services beyond writing and placing ads in newspapers and magazines on behalf of their clients. Years later, in the 1930s for example, ad agents went a step further in creating radio soap operas that were sponsored in their entirety by a single brand. Thus, the brand name of the sponsor and the name of the program became inseparable (e. g., Lux Radio Theatre or the Kraft Music Hall). In the early years of the soap opera, advertising agencies typically wrote both programming and the ads.

7. The Birth of the Slogan

Advertisements consisting of a central catchy phrase or slogan became the mode in the 1890s. [...] The use of slogans as the focus of poster and newspaper advertising represented a break with the earlier technique of using long, wordy copy to explain the product and why the consumer should purchase it. Slogans focused instead on a single big idea expressed in the form of a memorable phrase, and ads using them often did not give "reasons why" to consumers. [...]

Fascination with slogans continues into contemporary advertising. Geico famously encourages potential customers to switch brands of automobile insurance with the slogan, *So Easy a Caveman Can Do It.* Nike's *Just Do It* is not only well-known but a part of contemporary popular culture. The long-running campaign *got milk*? is one of the most memorable slogans in recent advertising history. Such phrases are so catchy that they are easily remembered, frequently repeated, and often parodied.

8. The Emergence of Brands

[...] The advent of packaged goods — a box of salt, a bag of rice, and a pound of coffee with a brand name on it — changed marketing forever. Rice was no longer just rice, and coffee wasn't just coffee. [...]

What exactly is a brand? [...] brands have material markers — names, logos, and unique packaging and designs. But beyond these essential physical attributes, over time a brand acquires a history, a reputation, and a meaning to consumers. In other words, it takes on a "personality".

As brands emerged in the late 1800s in America, advertising played a significant role in imbuing commodities with specific meanings. Ivory soap was no longer called "white soap" but had its own name. It had a distinctive appearance, logo, and package design that hasn't changed much over the years. Other soaps and cleaning products were also some of the earliest successful brands. Pears' soap, a competitor to Ivory, was promoted with romantic images of perfect people in a dreamy world.

Today, advertising is largely the business of promoting brands. On some few occasions, advertisements introduce a new brand. Most of the time, however, contemporary advertising promotes an established brand—by encouraging loyalty among current users and attempting to persuade those who aren't users to switch brands.

9. Advertising to Women

The term consumer has a gender in the English language and it is feminine that became the operating principle of advertising in the early 20th century. Along with this went the knowledge that 80% or more of consumer purchases — except for big ticket items like appliances, automobiles, and homes — were made by women. Most key employees of advertising agencies until about 1950 were (white, protestant) men while women held jobs like receptionists and secretaries. Today, more than half the employees in American advertising agencies are women.

In these early years of stricter gender roles, men were *advertisers*, and women were *consumers*. Thus, when advertising spoke to consumers, it usually did so with the voice of male authority. Stuart Ewen, who explored the role of advertisers in the early 20th century in *Captains of Consciousness* (1976), tells how advertising offered women labor saving devices like washing machines and at the same time instructed them in their proper domestic roles as mothers and homemakers. It was not until the rebirth of feminism in the 1970s that advertising began to let women speak for themselves, use women as authority figures, and employ women in decision-making and creative roles in the advertising industry.

10. Broadcasting Advertisements

Radio stations were up and running in the world's major cities by the late 1920s. [...] The United States [...] immediately allowed radio to become a commercial medium with minimal government regulation. Few innovations transformed the nature of advertising as fundamentally as radio. Only television and the Internet would prove so revolutionary.

Radio liberated advertising from its relationship to literacy by communicating through music, jingles, and the spoken word. Advertising agencies were skeptical at first, but soon radio became their newest medium and advertising explored is seemingly endless possibilities. [...]

11. Television and Commercials

Commercial television developed after World War II. By the late

1940s, cities like New York, Chicago, and Los Angeles had functioning local television stations. By the early 1950s, three major networks (NBC, CBS, and ABC) supplied national programming. Most early broadcasts were live, in black-and-white, and aired only a few hours each night. It was not long, however, before TV antennas sprung up all over America. The country was fascinated with the new medium, although early television was often little more than "radio with pictures". [...] National commercials with high production values advertised widely distributed products while local commercials were generally low-budget operations. Reception was often poor. Even passing cars and household appliances generated static on early TV sets. Despite all this, the magic of TV was entertainment on a scale unknown before.

12. Advertising Globally

American advertising took an international turn around 1900 when American businesses looked to advertising agencies to help them sell their products abroad. [...] Lack of reliable information about local consumption habits and media opportunities made it difficult to manage advertising abroad in this manner. To remedy the problems, some American advertising agencies opened offices abroad to create more culturally appropriate ads and to manage media placement more effectively. However, most of these offices were forced to close during the Depression.

After World War II, major American agencies were on the move again — typically driven by their clients at home who wanted to do effective marketing of their products in foreign settings. Not only in Latin America but also in Australasia, South Africa, Western Europe, and the Middle East, American agencies opened branch offices. Top managers were frequently Americans, but copywriters, artists, and most other staff members were locals. This trend has continued and now involves more agencies and countries (for example, Russia, Eastern Europe, and Sub-Saharan countries). Corporate mergers of the 1980s and 1990s resulted in some mega-agencies, all of whom operate international and domestic offices to service their clients.

The push-and-pull of agency-client relations in the international arena has continually focused on the option of using the same ad everywhere (with only minor adjustments such as language spoken) versus the benefits of adjusting, even rethinking, strategies to better fit local customs and practices. Today markets cross national borders and international advertising is commonplace. Some corporations have used their advertising to create truly global brands — products whose identities bridge cultural and linguistic gaps on a wide scale. Coca-Cola, McDonald's, and Sony are examples.

13. Commercializing Cyberspace

The Internet became an essential part of American society in the 1990s. Computers replaced typewriters and email established itself as a necessity. Today, instantaneous communication with people everywhere is simple, and information on almost any topic is just a few keystrokes away.

Mass media began to decline with the advent of cable television in the 1970s. Until then, viewing options were limited and audiences were broad. Ads on cable, because of the proliferation of specialized programming, created more targeted groups of viewers with more narrowly defined interests. Broadcasting became *narrowcasting*, and advertising became more focused as well. Home and Garden channel viewers get advertisements for paint and other building products while Travel Channel viewers see ads for airlines and vacation spots.

The Internet narrows the aim further, not reaching households but targeting individuals. Marketers use Internet surfing habits to establish the interests and buying habits of individuals, making advertising more efficient. A *repersonalization* of messages is occurring — ironically bringing advertising back around to speaking more individually to potential customers.

But what does the future hold for advertising? As the world of corporations and advertising charts its future, the search for new advertising venues goes on. Advertising has been very innovative in the past in finding ways to communicate promotional messages. As technology has evolved, it has revolutionized advertising techniques as well as changing the social landscape. There is no reason to suspect that advertising will not continue to reinvent itself, discover new media, and develop new techniques — as it has done recently with viral marketing, social media, and mobile apps. Advertising as we know it may be at its end, but the culture of consumption is alive and well.

(Excerpted from William O'Barr's advertising course archive: "A Brief History of Advertising in the United States".)

References

Ewen, S. *Captains of Consciousness*. New York: McGraw-Hill, 1976.

Questions

1. How did advertising emerge? What are the socio-cultural factors that are related to the emergence and development of advertising?
2. What are the major strategies of advertising?
3. Why are feminist critics so concerned for advertising?
4. How would you define advertising based on the description of the emergence and the development of advertising?

Passage 2

Perspectives of Advertising

Advertising has been explored from various perspectives and thus has various definitions. In the following part are presented major views of advertising.

1. Advertising as Art

As a social and cultural critic, Raymond Williams defines advertising as the "official art of modern capitalist society" (During, ed. 1993:334) and as the "*magic*: a highly organized and professional system of magical inducements and satisfactions" (Qtd. in During, ed. 1993:335) in his essay entitled "Advertising: The Magic System", based on his studying of the changes in society in capitalist industrialization and the rise of mass consumption. He associates the art of advertising to church painting in the middle ages when the artwork was sponsored by the aristocrats. And by the word "sponsorship", Williams highlights the relationship between the business corporations and the advertising institutions as well as the commercial activities between them which have a purpose of emphasizing "bringing the good things of life" (Qtd. in During, ed. 1993:335). Moreover, Williams is concerned for the institutionalization and professionalization of advertising as "persuasive art" to manipulate consumers for materialist purpose. Therefore, he is very interested in the possibilities of limiting and resisting this persuasive power.

2. Advertising as Education

Advertising is perceived as with the function of education in the history of its development, especially by the U. S. president Calvin

Coolidge (1872-1933). As he says,

> "We see that basically it is that of education. [...] It makes new thoughts, new desires, new actions. [...] Rightfully applied, it the method by which desire is created for better things"①.

He sees desire and the crucial element separating the civilized from the uncivilized:

> "The uncivilized make little progress because they have few desires. The inhabitants of our country are stimulated to new wants in all directions. In order to satisfy their constantly increasing desires, they necessarily expand their productive powers. They create more wealth because it is only by that method that they can satisfy their wants. It is constantly enlarging circle that represents the increasing circle of civilization"②.

To "civilize" people means to stimulate the desire and to create the myth of an autonomous individual capable of freedom of consumption in the capitalist society. In fact this "civilizing" power is important in relation to Karl Marx's 19th century prediction of workers' eventual revolution because of continuing conditions of poverty and exploitation. Two factors significantly lessen such a revolt in the 20th century West. One was to raise wages to turn workers into consumers. The other was

---

① Calvin Coolidge's lines are quoted in Frank Presbrey, 1961, The History and Development of Advertising, Westport, CN: Greenwood Press, 1961: 619.

② Ibid.

the power of advertising which motivated workers to increased productivity and to increased consumption. Here, for Coolidge, advertising opens up an economic dimension that increasingly identified free choice and the satisfaction of desires with consumption, linking the economic with the social.

3. Advertising as Manipulation

John Kenneth Galbraith, a Harvard economist and critic, defines advertising as manipulation. He put forward his view of advertising from economic perspective in *The Affluent Society* (1958), and sees advertising as manipulating the public by creating artificial needs and wants. Galbraith based his argument primarily on the consumer desire which he sees as linking production and consumption in capitalist society and thinks that increased production depends on the firms' response to the consumer preferences, and that the success of the economy is determined by the meeting of consumer desire. Thus, he thinks that, as a reverse model of the previous proposition, as the increased production is the ultimate goal of companies, there needs the existence of consumer desire. Thus, advertising is the strategy of marketing to create consumer desire in the affluent society, where consumers already feel contented. Due to this contentedness and the lack of urgent desire among consumers, advertising is needed to stimulate this craving for goods, encouraging consumers to perceive their new wants and desires for the goods — "Advertising creates craving for more elegant automobiles, more exotic food, more erotic clothing, more elaborate entertainment — indeed for the entire modern range of sensuous, edifying, and lethal desires". But as this desire for goods is merely created and aroused but advertising, Galbraith thinks advertising generates false need of goods and direct consumers toward buying the highly advertised products, which adds to the cost of commodities and the burden of consumers in consequence. Galbraith's economic exploration of the utilitarian role of advertising: the creating of consumer demand, the expansion of advertising expenditure and the proliferation of venues in which ads are delivered, is an effective critique of the capitalist control and exploitation of consumers, but he ignored the power of the symbolic message in ads.

4. Advertising as Culture

The symbolic/cultural examination of advertising has involved quite a number of critics in this line of thinking. Advertising is taken for a process of cultural production in promoting consumption. Raymond Williams was among the early writers to note the "cultural quality" of advertising for materialist function (In During, ed. 1993:335). Stuart Ewen's *Captain's Consciousness* (1976) pioneered in critiquing advertising as teaching women virtues of family life and creating the ways of living to promote consumption in the 1920s when the U. S. started to shift from the industrial capitalism to a consumption-oriented society. Stephen Fox in *The Mirror Makers* (1984) shows that advertising was a "primary, independent force in the molding of American culture and mores" in the 1920s, thus mirroring "deeper cultural tendencies" (Qtd. in Leiss et al. 1990:5). Moreover, a very important aspect of advertising is the appropriating of female images and of gender roles to promote consumption, as critiqued by Judith Williamson's *Decoding Advertisements* (1978), Erving Goffman's *Gender Advertisements* (1979), and Robert Goldman's *Reading Ads Socially* (1992), etc.

In fact, the symbolic/cultural aspect of advertising refers to the sign value of images and goods, which is explored by the French semiotician Roland Barthes as early as the 1950s in his *Image, Music, Text* (1977), showing how adverting uses symbolic images to represent social ideology for commercial persuasion. Concerning advertising as a symbolic art, Theodore Levitt once explains why cultural resources are appropriated to attract audience,

> Civilization is man's attempt to transcend his ancient animality: and this includes both art and advertising. [...] Both represent a persuasive and I believe universal characteristic of human nature — the human audience demands symbolic interpretation in everything it sees and knows. If it doesn't get it, it will return a verdict of "no interest" (Levitt, 1970: 87-89).

In Levitt' view, only when it contains symbolic message will advertising be effective enough to attract audience, as human audience tend to link advertising images to reality/life. Consequently, advertising constitutes the symbolic baggage of goods.

5. Advertising as Communication

Gillian Dyer in *Adverting as Communication* (1982) defines advertising as a medium transmiting messages to consumers. Holding advertising as "one of the greatest vehicles of social communication" (Leiss et. al. 1990: 1), other critics (Leiss et al.) see advertising as multi-folded: they examine advertising in both the symbolic (using cultural symbols to weave dreams) and the informative (the advertising as a medium of communication) aspect together with its market concern. And their definition highlights social-cultural manipulation of objects and people. As they specify,

> Advertising is not a business expenditure undertaken in the hope of moving some merchandise off the store shelves, but is rather an integral part of modern culture. Its creations appropriate and transform a vast range of symbols and ideas;

> its unsurpassed communicative powers recycle cultural models and references back through the networks of social interactions. This venture is unified by the discourse through and about objects, which bonds together images of persons, products, and well-being (Leiss et al., 1990:5).

In these critics' view, advertising encompasses the many and complex aspects of life in the capitalist society: mass media, the advertising agency, the evolution of the mode of economy and cultural production. And the advertising discourse is the convergence of power manipulation, showing how the economic, sociocultural and institutional power is strategically targeting at the audience through the "cultural frame for goods" — sets of images, values and forms of communication. In a word, advertising is viewed as both communication and manipulation.

6. Advertising as Mythmaking

Myths are amusing stories of gods, goddesses and heroes in a given culture which can go beyond time and sometimes pass across cultures. The powerful life of myths lies in its origin in our imagination or fantasy. Advertising is considered as a form of mythmaking by Sal Randazzo, in his *Mythmaking on Madison Avenue* (1993, pp. ix-1),

> Advertisers sell products by mythologizing them, by wrapping them in our dreams and fantasies. [...] Advertising is not simply in the business of "selling soap". [...] Advertising turns products into brands by mythologizing them — by humanizing them and giving them distinct identities, personalities, and sensibilities that reflect our own. [...] Advertising has discovered a powerful truth: Dreams sell.

Here, Randazzo discloses the dream character of advertising: associating products with characters, creating logo and fusing identities and personalities with it through branding — a process of characterization. And this feature of advertising can be clearly shown in the fantasized image of a clown of McDonalds, a character of happiness; the tough, strong individual of an imagined Marlboro cowboy in the American West; and the Coca-Cola logo which seems to bring about dreamy passion. Brands themselves are but dreams carved on products, which are then reimagined, bringing people the satisfaction of staying in the dream world and of having their ordinary life transformed through consuming the branded products.

To conclude, as advertising concerns so many dimensions of human life — social, cultural, economic, and even historical, it is virtually impossible to define advertising from any single perspective. In spite of its complexity, advertising is universal in its persuasive power: offering information to perspective consumers to promote consumption, with social ideals and cultural values woven to target at consumers. However, many ads are cultural-specific, offering different message in different cultural circumstances. In contemporary times, with the development of technology, advertising simply penetrates into the very personal aspect of human life (e. g. gender, identity) and influences our ways of thinking and living. This makes the medium of communication so intriguing and complicated as to demand more and further critical evaluation.

References

Bathes, R. *Image*, *Music*, *Text* , Edited by S. Heath. New York: Hill & Wang, 1977.

Dyer, G. *Advertising as Communication*. London: Methuen, 1982.

Ewen, S. *Captains of Consciousness*. New York: McGraw-Hill, 1976.

Fox, S. *The Mirror Makers*. New York: William Morror, 1984.

Galbraith, J. K. *The Affluent Society*. Boston: Houghton Mifflin, 1958.

Goffman, E. *Gender Advertisements*. New York: Harper and Row, 1979.

Goldman, R. *Reading Ads Socially*. New York: Routledge, 1992.

Levitt, T. "The Morality of Advertising." *Harvard Business Review*, 48, 1970.

Randazzo, S. *Mythmaking on Madison Avenue*. Chicago: Probus Publishing, 1993.

Williams, R. "Advertising: The Magic System." In *The Cultural Studies*, Edited by Simon During, London & New York: Routledge, 1993.

Williamson, J. *Decoding Advertisements*. London: Marion Boyars, 1978.

Questions

What do you think of advertising? Do you think advertising is art, education, culture, or myth? Present your view by giving examples.

Part II Approaches of Advertising: Semiotic and Content Analysis

The French cultural critic Roland Barthes considers that advertising creates and naturalizes mythic meanings — cultural values behind visual images. Through a semiotic analysis of the visual signs, Barthes discloses that the visual sign in advertising actually consists of two levels of meanings, with the intended meaning hidden in the second level of the structure of the sign, when the sign is contextually situated. Thus, for Barthes, advertising is a form of cultural representation, through which the products are endowed with certain mythic meanings, namely, bourgeois ideology and ways of life, to be promoted to consumers. And consuming the products means consuming the ideological values and the bourgeois ways of life, which will in turn be maintained and perpetuated through the process of consumption. The following part is Roland Barthes' enunciation of his view on advertising, which is itself an illustration of semiotic analysis of advertising.

Passage 3

Myth Today

What is a myth, today? I shall give at the outset a first, very simple answer, which is perfectly consistent with etymology: *myth is a type of speech* ①.

1. Myth Is a Type of Speech

Of course, it is not *any* type: language needs special conditions in order to become myth: we shall see them in a minute. But what must be firmly established at the start is that myth is a system of communication, that it is a message. This allows one to perceive that myth cannot possibly be an object, a concept, or an idea; it is a mode of signification, a form. Later, we shall have to assign to this form historical limits, conditions of use, and reintroduce society into it: we must nevertheless first describe it as a form.

---

① Innumerable other meanings of the word "myth" can be cited against this. But I have tried to define things, not words.

It can be seen that to purport to discriminate among mythical objects according to their substance would be entirely illusory: since myth is a type of speech, everything can be a myth provided it is conveyed by a discourse. Myth is not defined by the object of its message, but by the way in which it utters this message: there are formal limits to myth, there are no "substantial" ones. Everything, then, can be a myth? Yes, I believe this, for the universe is infinitely fertile in suggestions. Every object in the world can pass from a closed, silent existence to an oral state, open to appropriation by society, for there is no law, whether natural or not, which forbids talking about things. A tree is a tree. Yes, of course. But a tree as expressed by Minou Drouet is no longer quite a tree, it is a tree which is decorated, adapted to a certain type of consumption, laden with literary self-indulgence, revolt, images, in short with a type of social *usage* which is added to pure matter.

Naturally, everything is not expressed at the same time: some objects become the prey of mythical speech for a while, then they disappear, others take their place and attain the status of myth. Are there objects which are *inevitably* a source of suggestiveness, as Baudelaire suggested about Woman? Certainly not: one can conceive of very ancient myths, but there are no eternal ones; for it is human history which converts reality into speech, and it alone rules the life and the death of mythical language. Ancient or not, mythology can only have an historical foundation, for myth is a type of speech chosen by history: it cannot possibly evolve from the "nature" of things.

[...]

Let me therefore restate that any semiology postulates a relation between two terms, a signifier and a signified. This relation concerns objects which belong to different categories, and this is why it is not one of equality but one of equivalence. We must here be on our guard for despite common parlance which simply says that the signifier *expresses* the signified, we are dealing, in any semiological system, not with two, but with three different terms. For what we grasp is not at all one term after the other, but the correlation which unites them: there are, therefore, the signifier, the signified and the sign, which is the associative total of the first two terms. Take a bunch of roses: I use it to *signify* my passion. Do we have here, then, only a signifier and a signified, the roses and my passion? Not even that: to put it accurately, there are here only "passionified" roses. But on the plane of analysis, we do have three terms; for these roses weighted with passion perfectly and correctly allow themselves to be decomposed into roses and passion: the former and the latter existed before uniting and forming this third object, which is the sign. It is as true to say that on the plane of experience I cannot dissociate the roses from the message they carry, as to say that on the plane of analysis I cannot confuse the roses as signifier and the roses as sign: the signifier is empty, the sign is full, it is a meaning. Or take a black pebble: I can make it signify in several ways, it is a mere signifier; but if I weigh it with a definite signified (a death sentence, for instance, in an anonymous vote), it will become a sign. Naturally, there are between the signifier, the signified and the sign, functional implications (such as that of the part to the whole) which are so close that to analyses them may seem futile; but we shall see in a moment that this distinction has a capital importance for the study of myth as semiological schema.

Naturally these three terms are purely formal, and different contents can be given to them. Here are a few examples: for Saussure, who worked on a particular but methodologically exemplary semiological system — the language or *langue* — the signified is the concept, the signifier is the acoustic image (which is mental) and the relation between concept and image is the sign (the word, for instance), which is a concrete entity.① For Freud, as is well-known, the human psyche is a stratification of tokens or representatives. One term (I refrain from giving it any precedence) is constituted by the manifest meaning of behavior, another, by its latent or real meaning (it is, for instance, the substratum of the dream); as for the third term, it is here also a correlation of the first two: it is the dream itself in its totality, the parapraxis (a mistake in speech or behavior) or the neurosis, conceived as compromises, as economies effected thanks to the joining of a form (the first term) and an intentional function (the second term). We can see here how necessary it is to distinguish the sign from the signifier: a dream, to Freud, is no more its manifest datum than its latent content: it is the functional union of these two terms. In Sartrean criticism, finally (I shall keep to these three well known examples), the signified is constituted by the original crisis in the subject (the separation from his mother for Baudelaire, the naming of the theft for Genet); literature as discourse forms the signifier; and the relation between crisis and discourse defines the work, which is a signification. Of course, this tri-dimensional pattern, however constant in its form, is actualized in different ways: one cannot therefore say too often that semiology can have its unity only at the level of forms, not contents; its field is limited, it knows only one operation: reading, or deciphering.

In myth, we find again the tri-dimensional pattern which I have just described: the signifier, the signified and the sign. But myth is a particular system, in that it is constructed from a semiological chain which existed before it: it is a *second-order semiological system*. That which is a sign (namely the associative total of a concept and an image) in the first system, becomes a mere signifier in the second. We must

---

① The notion of word is one of the most controversial in linguistics. I keep it here for the sake of simplicity.

here recall that the materials of mythical speech (the language itself, photography, painting, posters, rituals, objects, etc.), however, different at the start, are reduced to a pure signifying function as soon as they are caught by myth. Myth sees in them only the same raw material; their unity is that they all come down to the status of a mere language. Whether it deals with alphabetical or pictorial writing, myth wants to see in them only a sum of signs, a global sign, the final term of a first semiological chain. And it is precisely this final term which will become the first term of the greater system which it builds and of which it is only a part. Everything happens as if myth shifted the formal system of the first significations sideways. As this lateral shift is essential for the analysis of myth, I shall represent it in the following way, it being understood, of course, that the spatialization of the pattern is here only a metaphor:

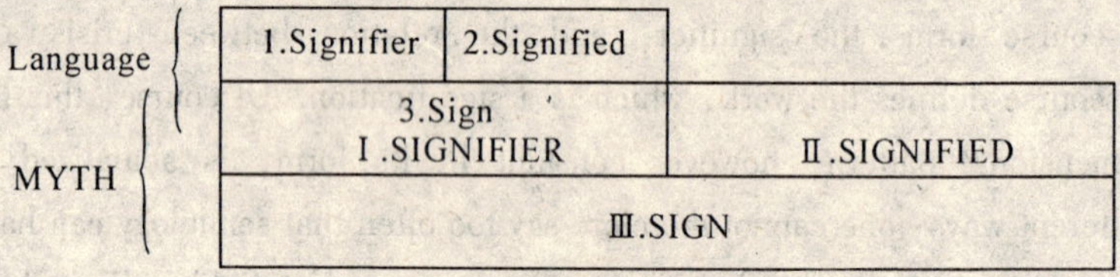

Roland Barthes, *Myhologies*

(1957, Trans. Annette Lavers, Vintage: London, 1993), 115

It can be seen in myth that there are two semiological systems, one of which is staggered in relation to the other: a linguistic system, the language (or the modes of representation which are assimilated to it), which I shall call the *language-object*, because it is the language which myth gets hold of in order to build its own system; and myth itself, which I shall call *metalanguage*, because it is a second language, in which one speaks about the first. When he reflects on a metalanguage, the semiologist no longer needs to ask himself questions about the composition of the language-object, he no longer has to take into account the details of the linguistic schema; he will only need to know its total term, or global sign, and only inasmuch as this term lends itself to myth. This is why the semiologist is entitled to treat in the same way writing and pictures: what he retains from them is the fact that they are both *signs*, that they both reach the threshold of myth endowed with the same signifying function, that they constitute one just as much as the other, a language-object.

[...]

Figure 1: *Paris-Match*, No. 326, 1955

Here is now another example [. . .]: I am at the barber's, and a copy of *Paris-Match* is offered to me. On the cover, a young Negro in a French uniform is saluting, with his eyes uplifted, probably fixed on a fold of the tricolour. All this is the *meaning* of the picture. But, whether naively or not, I see very well what it signifies to me: that France is a great Empire, that all her sons, without any colour discrimination, faithfully serve under her flag, and that there is no better answer to the detractors of an alleged colonialism than the zeal shown by this Negro in serving his so-called oppressors. I am therefore again faced with a greater semiological system: there is a signifier, itself already formed with a previous system (*a black soldier is giving the French salute*); there is a signified (it is here a purposeful mixture of Frenchness and militariness); finally, there is a presence of the signified through the signifier. [. . .] In myth (and this is the chief peculiarity of the latter), the signifier is already formed by the signs of the language. [. . .] Myth has in fact a double function: it points out and it notifies, it makes us understand something and it imposes it on us. [. . .]

One must put the biography of the Negro in parentheses if one wants to free the picture, and prepare it to receive its signified. [. . .] The form does not suppress the meaning, it only impoverishes it, it puts it at a distance. [. . .] It is this constant game of hide-and-seek between the meaning and the form which defines myth. The form of myth is not a symbol: the Negro who salutes is not the symbol of the French Empire: he has too much presence, he appears as a rich, fully experienced, spontaneous, innocent, *indisputable* image. But at the same time this presence is tamed, put at a distance, made almost transparent; it recedes a little, it becomes the accomplice of a concept which comes to it fully armed, French imperiality. [. . .]

Myth is [. . .] defined by its intention. [. . .] much more than by its literal sense. [. . .] In spite of this, its intention is somehow frozen, purified, eternalized, made absent by this literal sense (*The French Empire? It's just a fact: look at this good Negro who salutes like one of our own boys*). This constituent ambiguity... has two consequences for the signification, which henceforth appears both like a notification and like a statement of fact. [...] French imperiality condemns the saluting Negro to be nothing more than an instrumental signifier, the Negro suddenly hails me in the name of French imperiality; but at the same moment the Negro's salute thickens, becomes vitrified, freezes into an eternal reference meant to establish French imperiality. [...]

We reach here the very principle of myth: it transforms history into nature... In the case of the soldier-Negro [...] what is got rid of is certainly not French imperiality (on the contrary, since what must be actualized is its presence); it is the contingent, historical, in one word: *fabricated*, quality of colonialism. Myth does not deny things, on the contrary, its function is to talk about them; simply, it purifies them, it makes them innocent, it gives them a natural and eternal justification, it gives them a clarity which is not that of an explanation but that of a statement of fact. If I *state the fact* of French imperiality without explaining it, I am very near to finding that it is natural and *goes without saying*: I am reassured. In passing from history to nature, myth acts economically: it abolishes the complexity of human acts, it gives them the simplicity of essences, it does away with all dialectics, with any going back beyond what is immediately visible, it organizes a world which is without contradictions. [...] Things appear to mean something by themselves. [...]

2. Myth Is Depoliticized Speech

And this is where we come back to myth. Semiology has taught us that myth has the task of giving an historical intention a natural justification, and making contingency appear eternal. Now this process is exactly that of bourgeois ideology. If our society is objectively the privileged field of mythical significations, it is because formally myth is the most appropriate instrument for the ideological inversion which defines this society: at all the levels of human communication, myth operates the inversion of *anti-physis* into *pseudo-physis* .

What the world supplies to myth is an historical reality, defined, even if this goes back quite a while, by the way in which men have produced or used it; and what myth gives in return is a *natural* image of this reality. And just as bourgeois ideology is defined by the abandonment of the name "bourgeois", myth is constituted by the historical quality of things: in it, things lose the memory that they once were made. The world enters language as a dialectical relation between activities, between human actions; it comes out of myth as a harmonious display of essences. A conjuring trick has taken place; it has turned reality inside out, it has emptied it of history and has filled it with nature, it has removed from things their human meaning so as to make them signify a human insignificance. The function of myth is to empty reality: it is, literally, a ceaseless flowing out, a hemorrhage, or perhaps an evaporation, in short a perceptible absence.

It is now possible to complete the semiological definition of myth in a bourgeois society: *myth is depoliticized speech*. One must naturally understand *political* in its deeper meaning, as describing the whole of human relations in their real, social structure, in their power of making the world; one must above all give an active value to the prefix *de-*: here it represents an operational movement, it permanently embodies a defaulting. In the case of the soldier-Negro, for instance, what is got rid of is certainly not French imperiality (on the contrary, since what must be actualized is its presence); it is the contingent, historical, in one word: *fabricated* , quality of colonialism. Myth does not deny things, on the contrary, its function is to talk about them; simply, it purifies them, it makes them innocent, it gives them a natural and eternal justification, it gives them a clarity which is not that of an explanation but that of a statement of fact. If I *state the fact* of French imperiality without explaining it, I am very near to finding that it is natural and *goes without saying*: I am reassured. In passing from history to nature, myth acts economically: it abolishes the complexity of human acts, it gives them the simplicity of essences, it does away with all dialectics, with any going back beyond what is immediately visible, it organizes a world which is without contradictions because it is without depth, a world wide open and wallowing in the evident, it establishes a blissful clarity: things appear to mean something by themselves. ①

(From: *Mythologics* by Roland Barthes, translated by Annette Lavers, Hill and Wang, New York, 1984.)

Questions

1. What does it mean by "myth is a type of speech chosen history: it cannot possibly evolve from the 'nature' of things"?
2. What does "myth" refer to, according to Roland Barthes? Please explain specifically the linguistic character of "myth", from Saussure's semiotic perspective.
3. What is metalanguage? How do you understand in the two semiological systems of myth?
4. Concerning the little black boy's saluting on the cover of *Paris*-Match, what is the mythic speech there? How do you analyze it?
5. How do you understand "It is this constant game of hide-and-seek between the meaning and the form which defines myth" (in Para. 9)?

① To the pleasure-principle of Freudian man could be added the clarity-principle of mythological humanity. All the ambiguity of myth is there: its clarity is euphoric.

How do you understand the "intention" and the "constituent ambiguity" (in Para. 10) of the characteristics of myth? Does the form, the saluting black boy, mean transparently? What knowledge is a necessity to capture the concept of the image?

6. What other characteristics of myth are assumed in Paragraph 11, especially in the following sentences:
   "In passing from history to nature, myth acts economically: it abolishes the complexity of human acts, it gives them the simplicity of essences, it does away with all dialectics, with any going back beyond what is immediately visible, it organizes a world which is without contradictions. [...] Things appear to mean something by themselves..."?
7. What does it mean by "myth is depoliticized speech"?

Passage 4

Rhetoric of the Image

According to an ancient etymology, the word *image* should be linked to the root *imitari*. Thus we find ourselves immediately at the heart of the most important problem facing the semiology of images: can analogical representation (the "copy") produce true systems of signs and not merely simple agglutinations of symbols? It is possible to conceive of an analogical "code" (as opposed to a digital one)? We know that linguists refuse the status of language to all communication by analogy — from the "language" of bees to the "language" of gesture — the moment such communications are not doubly articulated, are not founded on a combinatory system of digital units as phonemes are. Nor are linguists the only ones to be suspicious as to the linguistic nature of the image; general opinion too has a vague conception of the image as an area of resistance to meaning — this in the name of a certain mythical idea of Life: the image is re-presentation, which is to say ultimately resurrection, and, as we know, the intelligible is reputed antipathetic to lived experience. Thus from both sides the image is felt to be weak in respect of meaning: there are those who think that the image is an extremely rudimentary system in comparison with language and those who think that signification cannot exhaust the image's ineffable richness. Now even — and above all if — the image is in a certain manner the *limit* of meaning, it permits the consideration of a veritable ontology of the process of signification. How does meaning get into the image? Where does it end ? And if it ends, what is there *beyond* ? Such are the questions that I wish to raise by submitting the image to a special analysis of the messages it may contain. We will start by making it considerably easier for ourselves: we will only study the advertising image. Why? Because in advertising the signification of the image is undoubtedly intentional; the signifieds of the advertising message are formed *a priori* by certain attributes of the product and these signifieds have to be transmitted as clearly as possible. If the image contains signs, we can be sure that in advertising these signs are full, formed with a view to the optimum reading: the advertising image is *frank* , or at least emphatic.

1. The Three Messages

Here we have a Panzani advertisement: some packets of pasta, a tin, a sachet, some tomatoes, onions, peppers, a mushroom, all emerging from a half-open string bag, in yellows and greens on a red background. Let us try to "skim off" the different messages it contains.

The image immediately yields a first message whose substance is linguistic; its supports are the caption, which is marginal, and the label, these being inserted into the natural disposition of the scene. [...] The code from which the message has been taken is none other

Figure 2

than that of the French language; the only knowledge required to decipher it is a knowledge of writing and French. In fact, this message can itself be further broken down, for the sign *Panzani* gives not simply the name of the firm but also, by its assonance, an additional signified, that of "Italianicity". The linguistic message is thus twofold (at least in this particular image): denotational and connotational. Since, however, we have here only a single *typical* ① sign, namely that of articulated (written) language, it will be counted as one message.

Putting aside the linguistic message, we are left with the pure image (even if the labels are part of it, anecdotally). This image straightaway provides a series of discontinuous signs. First (the order is unimportant as these signs are not linear), the idea that what we have in the scene represented is a return from the market. A signified which itself implies two euphoric values: that of the freshness of the products and that of the essentially domestic preparation for which they are destined. Its signifier

---

① By " *typical* " sign is meant the sign of system insofar as it is adequately defined by its substance: the verbal sign, the iconic sign, the gestural sign are so many typical signs.

is the half-open bag which lets the provisions spill out over the table, "unpacked". To read this first sign requires only a knowledge which is in some sort implanted as part of the habits of a very widespread culture where "shopping around for oneself" is opposed to the hasty stocking up (preserves, refrigerators) of a more "mechanical" civilization. A second sign is more or less evident; its signifier is the bringing together of the tomato, the pepper and the tricoloured hues (yellow, green, red) of the poster; its signified is Italy or rather *Italianicity*. This sign stands in a relation of redundancy with the connoted sign of the linguistic message (the Italian assonance of the name *Panzani*) and the knowledge it draws upon is already more particular; it is a specifically "French" knowledge (an Italian would barely perceive the connotation of the name, no more probably than he would the Italianicity of tomato and pepper), based on a familiarity with certain tourist stereotypes. Continuing to explore the image (which is not to say that it is not entirely clear at the first glance), there is no difficulty in discovering at least two other signs: in the first, the serried collection of different objects transmits the idea that of a total culinary service, on the one hand as though Panzani furnishes everything necessary for a carefully balanced dish and on the other hand as though the concentrate in the tin were equivalent to the natural produce surrounding it; in the other sign, the composition of the image, evoking the memory of innumerable alimentary paintings, sends us to an aesthetic signified: the "*nature mort*" ① or, as it is better expressed in other languages, the "still life"; the knowledge on which this sign depends is heavily cultural. [...]

[...]

If our reading is satisfactory, the photograph analyzed offers us

① "*nature morte*": In French, the expression refers to the original presence of funereal objects, such as a skull, in certain pictures.

three messages: a linguistic message, a coded iconic message, and a non-coded iconic message. The linguistic message can be readily separated from the other two, but since the latter share the same (iconic) substance, to what extent have we the right to separate them? It is certain that the distinction between the two iconic messages is not made spontaneously in ordinary reading: the viewer or the image receives at one and the same time the perceptual message and the cultural message. [...]

If the distinction permits us to describe the structure of the image in a simple and coherent fashion and if this description paves the way for an explanation of the role of the image in society, we will take it to be justified. The task now is thus to reconsider each type of message so as to explore it in its generality, without losing sight of our aim of understanding the overall structure of the image, the final inter-relationship of the three messages. Given that what is in question is not a "*naïve*" ① analysis but a structural description, the order of the messages will be modified a little by the inversion of the cultural message and literal message; of the two iconic messages, the first is in some sort imprinted on the second: the literal message appears as the support of the "symbolic message". Hence, knowing that a system which takes over the signs of another system in order to make them its signifiers is a system of connotation, we may say immediately that the literal image is denoted and the symbolic image connoted. [...]

(Excerpted from Roland Barthes: *Image*, *Music*, *Text*, originally published in 1964. Edited by S. Heath, New York: Hill and Wang, 1977.)

---

① "*Naïve*" analysis is an enumeration of elements: structural description aims to grasp the relation of these elements by virtue of the principle of the solidarity holding between the terms of a structure: if one term changes, so also do the others.

Questions

1. What does the author say about the image?
2. Does an image in advertising have an objective meaning? What is the exact word used by the author?
3. What is the first message in the Panzani ad, according to Barthes? What is its signified?
4. What does Barthes say about the images? What are their signifieds? Do readers need knowledge of daily life or of their culture to decode the meanings of these images in the ad?
4. In the final paragraph, what are the three messages of the ad in Barthes' view? What is the "literal message"? And the "cultural message"? How are they related to the "symbolic message"?
5. How do you understand the "denoted" image and the "connoted" image?

Passage 5

Content Analysis

The weaknesses of semiology as a method of studying advertising messages can be largely overcome by using content analysis, which is derived from a social science tradition rather than from linguistics and literary criticism. The issue of reliability, the size of the data base, and generalization from a sample to a larger universe are specifically taken into account in the content analysis design.

The unit for analysis in both methods is identical — the single ad. Semiology can admittedly do a better job on the single ad in isolation, because it is explicitly concerned with the "movement" of meaning within the text and between the text and the outside world. Content analysis can do a little more than "unpack" the surface meaning of an ad in a rather obvious way; its strength stems from its ability to relate this information to the sample as a whole in a rigorous manner, and to detect patterns of similarities and differences.

"Content analysis is a research technique for the objective, systematic and quantitative description of the manifest content of communication" (Berelson, 1952: 15). Four points in this classic definition require expansion.

First, "objective description" implies that there should be an acceptable level of agreement among different analysts about how to interpret the materials in questions. Different researchers working with the same data, in other words, should arrive independently at the same descriptive classifications (or at least within allowable parameters for variations). In part, content analysis attempts to deal with the variations that inevitably appear when observations by various researchers are compared by controlling the context within which those observations take place. Thus, "objectivity" refers not only to the interpretation but also to the control of observations.

Second, "systematic description" means that the same set of criteria should be applied to all the data under examination. The semiologist goes looking for descriptive categories within the material under examination itself, but the content analyst arrives at the data fully armed with the descriptive categories to be used, and can add no others later. This provides a basis for comparison and sorting within a data set. Content analysis is also systematic in that this data set is preselected sample of ads, chosen by recognized randomizing procedures, rather than by picking out "ideal types" that best display the characteristics the researcher regards as being of special significance.

Third, the descriptive categories employed in content analysis can be tied to specific quantitative procedures, permitting a degree of precision in measurement. The semiologist may hazard a guess about the relative preponderance of certain imagery in advertising, as in "women are often shown mentally drifting from the scene," but the content analyst is able to make more definite statements: "In 82% of ads sampled, women were coded as exhibiting the characteristic 'mentally drifting from the scene'." (Of course, the significance of this measurement can only be interpreted within the validity of the overall theoretical framework.)

Fourth, perhaps the most important point is that content analysis deliberately restricts itself to measuring the manifest or "surface" content of the message under study, for the simple reason that only in this respect can different investigators reach acceptable levels of agreement.

> The requirement of objectivity stipulates that only those symbols and combinations of symbols actually appearing in the message be recorded. In other words, at the *coding* stage of research, the stage at which specified words, themes, and the like are located in the text and placed into categories, one is limited to recording only those items which actually appear in the document. (Holsti, 1969:12)

There should be no reading between the lines: ideally, the account should be limited to what is apparent to everyone.

With these four points in mind, we shall review in detail the various elements of content analysis.

1. Theory

Although content analysis is considered an empirical approach, its starting point must always be theoretical. Just as in other scientific routines, the first step is to decide what to study; content analysis can only measure what one deems important to measure. The particular perspective from which one approaches the study of advertising or any other form of communication will generate the kinds of questions one asks.

[...]

2. Constructing Categories

The next step is to break the concept down so that we have a working tool for the detailed study of particular advertisements. (Sometimes the term "operationalization" is used to describe how a concept is turned into working tools for empirical research by "splitting it up" into representative categories. [...]

Two factors are of prime importance. First, we have to ensure that the categories we construct to measure the dimensions of concept are exhaustive; that is, they must cover all the dimensions relevant to the concept that exist in the material under study. Often the difficulties encountered at this point are overcome by creating the category of "other" into which all problematic cases are fitted. Second, the categories must be mutually exclusive; that is, any occurrence should fit into only one category. For example, if we are trying to measure the racial/ethnic typologies of characters appearing in commercials, and our categories of characters are (1) Black, (2) European, (3) Caucasian, and (4) American, we will not get useful results.

Constructing categories is the most critical and time-consuming state of content analysis, because in a very real sense the entire success of the enterprise depends on the coherence and appropriateness of the categories. Therefore, it is a good idea to pre-test the categories on a small sample of material and revise them, if necessary, to ensure that no major unexpected occurrences will complicate the coding stage later. [...]

The refining and redefinition of categories at this preliminary state also gives us the opportunity to guarantee the reliability of the coding protocol, that is, to check that the results will not be skewed by idiosyncratic readings. The usual procedure here is to compare the codings of one person with those of others, ensuring measures of consistency that will fall within certain accepted parameters.

3. Sampling

Now that we have developed our categories and tested the coding protocol, we must decide upon the "universe" that we want to study. We may be interested in the presentations of male and female roles in magazine ads from 1900 to 1984; if so, our universe will be "magazine ads from 1900 to 1984". [...] Defining the universe under analysis is important, because the generalizations we make on the basis of the study are applicable only to things within that specific universe.

Even when we have defined our universe, we will almost certainly not be able to examine every unit within it. For example, if we were interested in looking at role portrayals of men and women in prime-time television commercials over a span of one year, we would calculate the universe as follows: Prime time is 8:00 to 11:00 every evening, so the number of hours under study would be $3 \times 365 = 1,095$ hours for one network; on average at least twelve ads are shown every hour on network television, so our universe of ads for one year of prime-time television on one network would be $12 \times 1,095 = 13,140$.

It is unlikely that anyone would have the time, resources, and patience to analyze over 13,000 ads. Social scientists have devised sampling tables to help us select some fraction of our universe for actual study that will still let us have confidence in the generalizations we make about the whole. By using sampling tables, we can choose a smaller number of the items in the universe for actual study. In our example, 220 ads taken from the relevant time periods would satisfy the accepted conventions for sampling and reliability.

4. Coding

With a sample with the universe under consideration selected as our data base, we are in a position to start the actual analysis by applying the coding protocol to the ads in our sample. This can be done in a number of different ways in order to come up with data in a qualified form.

The most common is for the coder or coders to assign whatever is being measured to one of the categories that have been constructed. [...]

In some situations, we simply cannot choose one from a number of categories. For instance, to specify the racial types of people shown in ads in which more than one person or racial type appears, we would devise categories such as Black, Caucasian, Asian, Native Indian, Oriental, and so forth, and code such as either "absent" or "present." Here each category is treated as a separate variable that itself has two subcomponents (absent/present).

[...]

5. Analysis and Interpretation of Data

Depending on the size and complexity of the data set, the coding results may be analyzed by hand or run through computer routines. The researcher may then compare the numerical counts of the various categories under consideration; the process of giving statistical precision to unsystematic perceptions can be a very useful guideline for supporting hunches based on simple impressions.

Content analysis also allows the data to be recognized along some different dimensions, especially if the data have been entered into a computer. We might have been coding each ad for many different things at the same time: specifying gender, occupations, and racial types, for example, or the type of television show of magazine the ad appeared in, the type of product it advertised and its price range, other themes present, and so forth. Then, by cross-tabulating two or more of the variables, we start to see significant differentiations and patterns within the data. For example, we can tell whether different types of magazines consistently portray male and female roles in divergent ways.

The main purpose of this final stage should be to shed some light on the theoretical starting point of the project, which really frames and guides the entire process. The extent to which the subsequent procedures address this issue directly, enabling us to understand it better, is the measure of the success or failure of any exercise in content analysis.

6. Strengths and Weaknesses of Content Analysis

The great strength of content analysis for the study of advertisements is its ability to supply some objective answers to the question, "What is going on in these ads?" In this context, the term "objective" implies no more than "satisfactory intercoder reliability". It allows us to treat qualitative data in quantitative terms, thus helping ground our analysis of images and words in something more than individual and impressionistic interpretation. When dealing with large amounts of data, patterns that otherwise are difficult or impossible to detect often show up in content analysis procedures.

However, content analysis has been dismissed by many writers as being totally inadequate for the measurement of meaning. They claim that meaning cannot be captured when communication is broken down into discrete categories of form and content, for meaning is dependent upon the place of any particular item within an entire system of language and image. Isolating any one element alters the meaning not only of that element itself, but also the meaning of the whole structure.

Colin Sumner maintains that content analysis puts too much emphasis on the "repeatability" of signs (that is, the number of times they occur), and too little on their significance for the audience. No matter how often something appears in the message system, if the reader or viewer cannot understand it, then the repetition is irrelevant: "It is not the significance of repetition that is important but the repetition of significance." Because content analysis does not pose questions about the meaning of items within a message, the repetitions it detects have no understandable context: "The absence of a theory of signs, signification, and significance renders content analysis absurd because its key concept is left unsupported and that concept gives it no knowledge of its avowed object, the content!" (Sumner, 1979: 69)

Sumner's point is that content analysis can say nothing about the audience's interpretation of the message because it has no theory of signification. But this is not necessarily a weakness, as long as one does not try to use it to demonstrate the effect on the audience. For, while content analysis cannot tell us anything about how audiences may be "reading" messages, it can tell us a good deal about what went into the construction of those messages. However, we also know that advertisers are on very familiar term with their audiences, and that they spend a great deal of time and effort in learning how audiences decode messages. On this basis, we can say with some assurance that most aspects of modern advertising are meaningful to their intended audiences.

The real weakness in content analysis, especially for the study of advertising, lies in its restricted range of application. As we have seen, it can deal only with manifest content, that is, the surface or denotative level of messages. Modern advertising, especially in the age of market segmentation, works at important connotative levels of communication with multiple levels of meaning. Most ads today have a latent meaning that we are asked to "fill in" and thus participate in completing the message.

(Excerpted from: Leiss, Kline, & Jhally, S. *Social Communication in Advertising*. Ontario: Nelson Canada, 1990.)

References

Berelson, B. *Content Analysis in Communication Research*. New York: Free Press, 1952.

Holsti, O. *Content Analysis for the Social Sciences and Humanities*. Reading, Mass: Addison-Wesley, 1969.

Sumner, C. *Reading Ideologies*. London: Academic, 1979

Questions

1. Why is content analysis important in analyzing advertisements?
2. What are the differences between semiotic analysis and the content analysis?
3. What are the major steps of content analysis?
4. What is the disadvantage of content analysis?
5. Please read the example of content analysis in the Supplementary Materials and see how content analysis is conducted to analyze magazine advertising.

Chapter 2　Body and Power

Introduction

The advertising critic Sut Jally points out in *The Codes of Advertising* (1990) that advertising mostly appropriate female images for symbolic and commercial promotion. William O'Barr (1994) also notes in the history of advertising that the "feminine" has been constructed in advertising and women have been targeted as the consumer in much of the advertising in the 20th century. For one thing, Betty Friedan (1963) discloses the "feminine mystique" constructed by the media and advertising in the 1950s to encourage the post-war white women to return to the family as male subordinates. With the Women's Liberation Movement and since the 1990s, feminists have been concerned for the predominant representation of the slim, female body in advertising and the adverse effects upon mass women. In fact, the critics have found that in advertising of the consumer society, the female body is almost the most favorable realm of cultural inscription and cultural contestation, as a spectacle, a commodity, an object of male control, as well as a site of women's resistance.

So the first subject of advertising studies is the critique of the economic and cultural power upon the female body. Articles of critics are introduced to inspire problematization of the gendered body in binary structure, to critique the media stimulation of body maintenance, the reification and commodification of the human body, especially the female one. Then, feminist critiquing of body discourse as power normalization is introduced to show power control from poststructualist point of view. Furthermore, Foucault's view of power as intertwining with resistance (1980) is introduced to confirm the possibility of decolonizing power. Finally, Ding's (2007) study testifies the changes in representing the female body in advertising due to the feminist resistance and women's self-empowering.

Part I Gender, Body, Self

Passage 1

Gendered Bodies

Traditional Western interpretations of the body construct just two, mutually exclusive, biological sexes based on their reproductive functions. The differences between male and female are innately grounded in reproduction metaphors, with explanations proceeding from a seemingly scientific biologically functional foundation.

However, the two-sex model of the human body has been in fashion only for the last few hundred years. Before that, there was a one-sex model. The female body was considered just an inferior version of the male. The utilization of a one-gender model, supposedly without attributing inherent female inferiority, is still available for many contemporary social processes, as in the case of unisex fashion and gender-neutral labor. On the other hand, several Native American cultures envision a three-gender model. In general, when it comes to determining the categories of sexual beings, there is a whole spectrum of fragments, variations, and projections.

Feminist analyses of both the body and gender constructions of the body focus on how power relations within social systems affect the "reality" of the body. Initially, those interpretations of the body were a political issue as feminists struggled to gain control over women's fertility and their right to abortion. Their analysis of gender and power also investigated how scientific discourse conceptualized both women's and men's bodies.

As has been discussed in section one, the Cartesian mind/body dualism divides human experience into a bodily realm and a consciousness realm. Feminist critiques of the Cartesian dualism illuminate how the female body is used exclusively as the metaphor for the corporeal pole of the dualism. The female body represents nature (Mother Nature), emotionality, irrationality, and sensuality. The dangerous, appetitive female body is seen as ruled by emotions, standing in contrast to the masterful, masculine will, the locus of social power, rationality, and self-control (Gowaty, 1997). In this comparison, the female body is always "other", mysterious and unruly.

The topics of feminist social theory of the body are as diverse as are the disciplines and methodologies with which they are analyzed. From hysteria and "rest cures" in the 19th century to the recent focus on PMS, anorexia nervosa, and menopause, feminist analysis explores how and why women's bodies have been constructed as more susceptible to pathologies than their male counterparts. Feminist scholars have explored women's sexual desire and experiences, focusing specifically on how heterosexual norms have constrained understandings of the body. Women's experiences with the appearance of their bodies have been investigated, analyses ranging from the more routine beauty practices, fitness regimes, and fashion to dieting, female eating disorders, and cosmetic surgery. Representations of female body in film and on television have been examined, showing how cultural images in the media set standards for women by presenting images of "desirable" female bodies as seductive, white, affluent, and thin.

Overall, feminist scholarship is critical of the two-sexed biological foundation underlying much of Western thought. Simone de Beauvoir's famous statement in the 1950s that "Women are made, not burn", launched a whole generation of feminist scholars focused on challenging the doctrine of "natural difference" (de Beauvoir, 1989). Feminists have sought to demonstrate how gender is socially, not biologically, constructed. Contesting women as "natural mothers", "naturally less aggressive", "naturally weaker", feminist interpretations of the female body focus on the power of cultural mandates to legitimate gendered relations of domination and subordination.

Recently, feminist scholarship has begun to analyze the suppositions behind even this sex/gender distinction. While challenging the assumed basic nature of the two-sexed body guiding much of contemporary research, current analyses also illuminate how heterosexuality has been another hidden assumption of past research. This current scholarship shows how, even in academic research, the taken-for-granted nature of heterosexuality has bolstered both the foundations and the distinctions between male and female.

Judith Butler has been highly influential in breaking the boundaries of interpretation around notions of differences between a biologically sexed and socially constructed gender. She challenges the assumption that genitals define the boundary between two sexes and two genders. Instead, she suggests each individual body enacts and can be read as a "gender performance" (Butler, 1990). How do you know if a person is female or male? The daily performances supported through appropriate costumes, hairstyles, and bodily actions such as ways of sitting, standing, and talking all generate easily read binary distinctions between men and women. Attacking the binary thought process inherent in the two-sexed model, theorists like Butler are now celebrating the transgressive nature of performance and display inherent in bodybuilding, the male transvestite, and the early performances of Madonna. Butler suggests that looking at the performances inherent in these "gender-troubled" arenas illuminates the daily performances we all act out to display Western assumptions of appropriate gender roles.

Body image within a system of patriarchy has traditionally been perceived as a woman's issue. While women's concern for appearance is linked to female sex-role stereotypes, until recently, the role that physical appearance and body image play for men has been ignored. From the flapper of the Roaring Twenties to the buxom Marilyn Monroe in the 1950s to the waiflike thinness of Twiggy in the 1960s, images of women's bodies have been symbolic icons and markers of decades. Yet, an examination of women's bodies which excludes men's relationship to their bodies tends to support and reproduce the Cartesian dualism of mind/man, body/women. Assuming men are above or beyond having a relationship with their bodies assumes men are just minds without bodies.

A review of current magazines and the media, however, suggests a celebration and focus on a young, lean, and muscular male body (Mishkind, 1987: 37). Men now serve as marketing targets for diet sodas, light beers, health spas, and reconstructive surgery. In his article in this section, Marc Mishkind suggests that with the collapse of other historical social values there has been a shift in emphasis towards men and their consumption habits, with an increased focus on their commodified appearance. Men may focus on different aspects of their bodies and discuss their bodies with a different vocabulary, but their various body parts are now being made into objects of commodification.

The increased attention to men's physical appearance, clothing, and "beautification" does not imply any relaxation of the pressure on women to conform. Viewed in combination, this trend seems to suggest there might develop an "equal objectification" of males. If women increasingly were to see and respond to men as men have traditionally responded to women, the change, while it might represent a kind of equalization, would not be a very satisfactory one. Males would then have to share the burden of coercion imposed by appearance norms. But it is by no means clear that the similar burden on women would thereby be removed or even reduced (Schur, 1987:61).

Men's Studies is concerned with many of these issues, and like its counterpart in Women's Studies, focuses on gender/sex as a problematic body construct. In conjunction with Women's Studies, Men's Studies also demonstrates that the differences between the sexes are small in comparison to the variations within them, and between cultural and historical situations. For example, there are cultural situations where rape is nonexistent or extremely rare, where the male is not aggressive, where homosexuality is expected within the life cycle, where mothers are not the primary caregivers.

One concept explored in Men's Studies is the social construction of masculinity. As with femininity, masculinity is traditionally thought to emerge from the body. It is supposedly inherent in a male body or is supposed to express the drives of a male body. And as half of the binary gender concept, masculinity is also defined by what it is not. It is a relational concept such that boys learn to be men through learning not to be women (Kimmel, 1987:15). Men are to avoid all "sissy" stuff and feminine behaviors. To be masculine is to act and look differently from women.

The body of the athlete is considered the ideal masculine body type. The athletic male body epitomizes competition and hierarchy among men, and the domination of women. Yet, this construction of gender becomes contested and questionable when the performance cannot be sustained, when for example, female athletes surpass a man's performance, when a man is injured or becomes chronically ill, or if a man is inept or never plays sports.

It is suggested that the increased cultural attention given to the male body and the increased demand placed on men to achieve a mesomorphic or muscular build is pushing men further along the continuum of bodily concern, with more joining the population of women with eating disorders (Mishkind, 1987:44). Men feel ashamed when they focus on their bodies, presumably because this has been associated traditionally with the female sex-role stereotype (Mishkind, 1987:44). Living within the male/female dualism, a masculine man should not be concerned with body image issues.

Interestingly, the new information technology industry and the sedentary work necessary for proficient computer use undercuts the traditional construction of masculinity and the body-as-machine connection. Indeed, the image of the computer nerd's body is invariably male, white, late adolescent, and physically unattractive. Portrayed as pale with pimply skin and thick, unflattering spectacles, skinny, with poor fashion sense, and "soft" from too much physical inactivity and junk food, they are feminized as "wimps" but maintain some power through their technological prowess.

And these "wimps" become targets for advertisers. Marketing has attempted to redefine keyboard work as an arena for competition and power, an area of technological mastery over challenges. Computer games are constructed with hyper-masculine and hyper-feminine bodies conquering and subduing opponents. For more on this aspect of metaphors and the vicarious pleasures of playing with stereotypically gendered bodies, see Anne Balsamo's (1996) *Technologies of the Gendered Body*.

(Excerpted from: Jessica R. Johnston: "Social Bodies" in *The*

American Body in Context: An Anthology, Edited by Jessica R. Johnston, Scholarly Resources Inc., 2001.)

References

Butler, J. *Gender Trouble: Feminism and the Subversion of Identity.* New York: Routledge, 1990.

Beauvoir, S. de. *The Second Sex.* New York: Vintage Press (Originally Published, 1952), 1989.

Gowaty, P. A. *Feminism and Evolutionary Biology: Boundaries, Intersections, and Frontiers.* New York: Chapman & Hall, 1997.

Kimmel, M. "Rethinking 'Masculinity'". In *Changing Men.* Edited by Kimmel, M. Beverly Hills: Sage Publications, 1987.

Mishkind, Marc. "The Embodiment of Masculinity." In *Changing Men*, Edited by Kimmel, M. Beverly Hills: Sage Publications, 1987.

Schur, W. "Women and Appearance Norms". In *Deviance: The Interactionist Perspective.* New York: Macmillan, 1987.

Questions

1. What does the female body represent in Cartisian dualism? How about the male body?
2. According to the author, what are the basic feminist concerns in terms of body and gender?
3. Judith Butler is especially concerned for the "gender trouble" and proposes the body as the site of "gender performance". Why does the author refer to "gender performance" as "transgressive"? What is transgressed?
4. What is wrong with today's media and the images of women, according to the author?
5. How were men and women conventionally represented in the media?
6. What is the new image of men?

7. Is Men's Studies also a feminist issue? Why?
8. How do you understand "the body-as-machine" metaphor and the construction of masculinity?

Passage 2

The Construction of the Body

> Stay young, stay beautiful, live longer. These are the catch phrases of today's hard living society... While the secret of longer life is still a long-way off, many people are searching for a short-cut — through health foods, yoga, gardening. Grab your survival kit and live longer. (The *Sun*)

Body maintenance cannot of course be claimed as a novel creation of consumer culture. In traditional societies, religious communities such as monasteries demanded ascetic routines with an emphasis upon exercise and dietary control (Turner, 1982). The adoption of ascetic regimes usually meant, however, that the body was subordinated to "higher" spiritual ends. The dominant ethos of Christianity was to denigrate and repress the human body. Jesuits were taught on entering the order to accept Ignatius Loyola's maxim Perinde ac cadaver (henceforth as a corpse) (Benthall, 1976: 69) The Christian tradition glorified an aesthetics of the soul, not the body. Ascetic regimes would release the spirit and subdue the sexual side of the body. Within consumer culture, on the other hand, sexual experts proclaim that dietary control and exercise will enhance sexual prowess; exercise and sexuality are blurred together through neologisms such as "sexercise" and "exersex". The shame in the naked body gradually gave way under the persistent critique of sexual experts and commercial interests. To enjoy heightened pleasure individuals have not only to consult the sexual manual and resort to a growing range of pills, aids, and devices, they must look good, too. Self-surveillance through taking instant pictures and videotapes celebrated sexual aesthetics: the naked body or the body packed in erotic sexual leisurewear could be recorded as proof of the achievement of a desired effect (Hepworth & Featherstone, 1982).

The term "body maintenance" indicates the popularity of the machine metaphor for the body. Like cars and other consumer goods, bodies require servicing, regular care, and attention to preserve maximum efficiency. ① As the consumption of goods increases, the time required for care and maintenance increases, and the same instrumental rational orientation adopted towards goods is turned inwards onto the body. The tendency to transform free time into maintenance work imposes even greater demands on the individual and makes the monitoring of the current state of bodily performance essential if individuals are to get the most out of life: the hectic life increases the need for "human servicing" (Linder, 1970: 40).

Preventive medicine offers a similar message and through its offshoot, health education, demands constant vigilance on the part of the individual who has to be persuaded to assume responsibility for his health. Introducing the category "self-inflicted illness," which results from body abuse (overeating, drinking, smoking, lack of exercise, etc.), health educationalists assert that individuals who conserve their bodies through dietary care and exercise will enjoy greater health and live longer. The calculation of the potential saving to state health services provides further grounds for castigating those who do not heed the new message as self-indulgent "slobs" (Featherstone & Hepworth, 1980, 1981; Hepworth & Featherstone, 1982). In effect, the health education

---

① See for example O. Gillie (1978), *The Sunday Times Book of Body Maintenance*, Diagram Group (1977), *Man's Body: An Owner's Manual*.

movement is trying to bring about a change in the moral climate so that individuals assume increasing self-responsibility for their health, body shape, and appearance. To some extent, this can be seen as building on and accentuating self-help tendencies which were present within the Victorian middle-class whose preoccupation with health matters led them to diet, take pills, take up athletics, etc. (Haly, 1979) Yet however much health educationalists appeal to the rationality of self-preservation and offer the incentives of longevity and lowered risk of disease, their body maintenance messages are strongly influenced by the consumer culture idealization of youth and the body beautiful. In the late 1970s, the British Health Education Council found that the most effective advertising message was to highlight the cosmetic rewards of fitness and dietary care. Health educationalists have little time for the health food crank or the fitness fanatic in their advertisements; these are discarded in favor of images of men and women who maximize, who get more out of life, who "look good and feel great," who are more attractive and therefore socially acceptable. Within this logic, fitness and slimness become associated not only with energy, drive, and vitality but worthiness as a person; likewise the body beautiful comes to be taken as a sign of prudence and prescience in health matters.

The popular media and commercial interests have found the "looking good and feeling great" health education message to be a saleable commodity. Eager to endorse body maintenance as a part of the consumer lifestyle, popular newspapers like the *Sun* and *Mirror* in Britain pass on the message to a wider audience with frequent articles on slimming, exercise, health foods and appearance. Center-page spreads enable readers to calculate their degree of success or failure in meeting age/height/weight targets and how to complete questionnaires to work out their "survival power." Feature articles on the calorific value of different types of food complement center-page spreads on the calorie burning power of different types of activity (running, sitting, walking, sleeping, kissing, sex, etc.), enabling the enterprising reader to draw up a daily calorific balance sheet to see if he or she can meet their designated target. In the last decade, there has also been a noticeable growth in the number of specialist magazines on jogging, running, health foods, exercise, and especially slimming. Self-help books on body maintenance also sell well: In December 1981 four out of ten books on the U. S. bestseller list were of the "how to lose weight" variety. Common to the popular media treatment of body maintenance, be it from the popular press, specialist magazines of the "Doctors' Answers" type, advertisements for vitamins, slimming products, or government health education propaganda, is the encouragement of self-surveillance of bodily health and appearance as well as the incentive of lifestyle benefits. Body maintenance is firmly established as a virtuous leisure time activity which will reap further lifestyle rewards resulting from an enhanced appearance: body maintenance in order to look good merges with the stylized images of looking good while maintaining the body. The images in the advertisements, popular press, and health education pamphlets are of lithe, bright-eyed, beautiful people, in varying states of nakedness, enjoy their body work. The fat are invariably portrayed as glum and downcast: joke figures, survivals from a bygone age.

One of the noticeable features of the twentieth century, according to Theodore Zeldin (1977:440), has been the triumph of the thin woman over fat woman. It can be added that in the second half of the 20th century this ideal is becoming firmly established for men, too, with the last bastions of corpulence amongst the working class now under siege. As the slim form becomes mandatory, almost every conceivable consumer product is discovered to have slimming properties. In 1931, the manufacturers of Lucky Strike cigarettes spent $19 million on advertising and successfully convinced many women that smoking was a vital aid to dieting (Susman, 1973:132). Today grapefruit juice, disco dancing, plankton, and sex are marketed with similar conviction. The beauty industry now offers "shapeovers" ("look 10 pounds slimmer without dieting")① to accompany "makeovers" as an essential part of every woman's cosmetic repertoire.

Within consumer culture slimness has become associated with health, and the health educational message that being overweight is a health risk has become absorbed into the conventional wisdom. Yet a good deal of the "advice" that abounds in the media and advertisements is clearly of a pseudoscientific nature. Rubin Andres has recently conducted an extensive review of a number of slimming studies and concluded that the overweight actually live longer. The age/height/weight charts originally constructed by insurance companies, which hang in doctors' surgeries and publicized in the popular media, are inaccurate—in some cases as much as fourteen pounds off. Andre's conclusion that slimness has little to do with health merely confirms those reached by earlier researchers such as Bruch (1957) and Beller (1977) and may be destined to have a similar lack of impact.

Women of course are well aware that the major reason for dieting is cosmetic and that "looking good" not only becomes necessary to achieve social acceptability but can become the key to a more exciting lifestyle. As one woman remarked in a slimming magazine article: "Being overweight was, for me, like living with the brakes on. And I *hated*

① The headline of a double-page spread in the *News of the World* magazine, *Sunday*, in January 1982. The text, surrounding a picture of a young woman in a leotard smiling as she exercised, referred to exercises devised by Adrian Arpel, "America's queen of self-improvement", the "boss of her own international cosmetics business" who claimed "anyone can shed ten pounds and ten years without a diet or facelift".

being held back." The lifestyle benefits are played up in slimming magazines and the popular press: not only do successful slimmers get more admiring glances, they feel more attractive and are confident to get out more, take up new exciting hobbies, and live out their version of the Martini people lifestyle (Hepworth & Featherstone, 1982).

Like slimming, jogging provides further insight into the transvaluation of use within consumer culture: everything has to be good for something else and the range of alleged benefits multiplies endlessly. Apart from reducing the chance of coronary heart disease, it is claimed jogging helps to cure impotence, increase confidence, psychological well-being, and puts "you in control of your body." Jogging has also been claimed to result in prolonged cosmetic benefits – improving posture, reducing stomach sag, helping to burn off excessive fat (Hepworth & Featherstone 1982: 107). The notion of running for running's sake, purposiveness without purpose, a sensuous experience in harmony with embodied and physical nature, is completely submerged amidst the welter of benefits called up by the market and health experts (Hepworth & Featherstone, 1982).

The instrumental strategies which body maintenance demands of the individual resonate with deep-seated features of consumer culture which encourage individual to negotiate their social relationships and approach their free time activities with a calculating frame of mind. Self-preservation depends upon the preservation of the body within a culture in which the body is the passport to all that is good in life. Health, youth, beauty, sex, fitness are the positive attributes which body care can achieve and preserve. With appearance being taken as a reflex of the self, the penalties of bodily neglect are a lowering of one's acceptability as a person, as well as an indication of laziness, low self-esteem, and even moral failure. Within consumer culture it is hardly surprising that aging and death are inevitable decay and defeat that are in store, even for the most vigilant of individuals. The secularization of the body has resulted in the eclipse of the traditional religious purpose of the body in which it was regarded as a transitory vehicle, a means to higher spiritual ends. Today, pain, suffering, and death are seen as unwelcome intrusions in the midst of a happy life (Ariès, 1974) and the consumer culture imagery has decreed that life can and should be everlastingly happy. Amidst images of comfort, fulfillment, and cleanliness, the unpleasant odors and sights surrounding death become intolerable: "the dirty death" (Ariès, 1981:568) has to be hidden away.

Within the limitation of its logic consumer culture is incapable of providing other than flawed solutions to the problems of aging and death. On the one hand it hides them away, suppresses them in the midst of illusions of endless hedonism, while flattering our vanity that we are enjoying the good life here and now. Yet it also needs to stimulate the fear of the decay and incapacities accompanying old age and death to jolt individuals out of complacency and persuade them to consume body maintenance strategies. In a feature article entitled "Have You the Looks That Last?" (day six of the *Sun* 's "Staying Alive Week" in June 1978) readers were warned:

> You may look sexy and beautiful now, but will you still be attractive when you're 50, 60, or even 70?
>
> To get the most out of life it makes sense to keep in tip-top shape in middle-age and beyond. Beauties like
>
> Joan Collins and Cyd Charisse believe that lasting good looks takes lots of hard work.

The illusion of technical mastery and even transcendence over the lifespan fits in well with the "calculating hedonism" (Jacoby, 1980:63) demanded by consumer culture. Within the "live for yourself " calculus, children are seen as bad investments in terms of time, money, and affection and even resented as possible rivals. Cars, jogging, tourism, self-actualization, and the new therapies offer more predictable pleasures and a better return on the investment of time and money (Jacoby, 1980:64). This suggests that within consumer culture a new relationship between the body and self has developed.

(Excerpted from: Mike Featherstone: "The Body in Consumer Culture" in *The American Body in Context: An Anthology*, Edited by Jessica R. Johnston, Scholarly Resources Inc., 2001.)

References

Ariès, P. T. *Western Attitudes Towards Death.* Baltimore: John Hopkins University Press, 1974.

Ariès, P. T. *The Hour of Our Death.* New York: Knopt, 1981.

Beller, A. S. *Fat and Thin: A Natural History of Obesity.* New York: Farrar, Strauss & Giroux, 1977.

Benthall, J. *The Body Electric: Patterns of Western Industrial Culture.* London: Thames and Hudson, 1976.

Bruch, H. *The Importance of Overweight.* New York: W Norton, 1957.

Featherstone, M & Hepworth, M. "Changing Images of Middle Age". In *Translations in Middle and Later Life*, Edited by M. Johnson. London: British Society of Gerontology, 1980.

Featherstone, M. & Hepworth, M. Images de la Maturité, *Gerontologie.* 1981, 12.

Haly, B. *The Healthy Body and Victorian Culture*, Cambridge, MA: Harvad UP, 1979.

Hepworth, M. & Featherstone, M. *Surviving Middle Age.* Oxford: Blackwell, 1982.

Jacoby, R. Narcissism and the Crisis of Capitalism, *Telos*, 1980, 44.

Linder, S. B. *The Harried Leisure Class*, New York: Columbia UP,

1970.

Susman, W. *Culture and Commitment* 1929-1945. New York: Braziller, 1973.

Zeldin, T. *France* 1948-1945, *Volume* 2: *Intellect*, *Taster and Anxiety*. Oxford: Oxford UP, 1977.

Questions

1. Why does the author say that body maintenance is not "a novel creation of consumer culture"? Has body been historically a space of freedom? Give examples to show your viewpoint based on the passage.
2. How do you understand the "machine metaphor" of the human body?
3. How does advertising make use of body maintenance message? What is the most effective advertising message according to the British Health Education Council?
4. What is the "saleable commodity"? How is it related to the human self?
5. Why does the author say that the "advice" that abounds in the ads is "clearly of a pseudoscientific nature"?
6. According to the author, how is body maintenance related to human personality?
7. Based on the viewpoints of this passage, how do you understand the notion of "self" in consumer culture? Is there an Enlightenmental notion of a self as an agent in consumer culture? Is the self absolute and stable? Is it an object to be molded?

Passage 3

The Reification and Commodification of the Body

Advertisements are not merely ways of communicating information about products. They are message systems designed to organize perceptions and "create structures of meaning" (Williams, 1968:12). They comprise framework through which a world of objects is translated into a world if social relationships with other people. Advertisers draw upon sociocultural meanings from both the viewers' life-worlds and the mass media. They then entwine these meanings into images that are returned to viewers — now framed in relation to products and services. This process is known as commodification, where advertisers turn a value, such as freedom, femininity, excitement, into a product or commodity that can purchased.

Commodification of the body turns the individual into an object composed of product-mediated parts — lips, eyes, waist, hips, hair, odors, and even clothes. Individuals become a means to display a collection of body parts, each serviced by appropriate products. The popular media and commercial interests have found that a body that both "looks good and feels great" is a very marketable commodity. Yet the portrayal of looking healthy collapses the experience of health with the mere presentation of health, suggesting that the attainment and /or the spectacle of a healthy body is available to be purchased across a wide variety of products.

A "healthy lifestyle" entails an entire category of consumer goods, binding together a set of consumption priorities with individual responsibility for that consumption. In a consumer culture, the commodification of health, of body maintenance, develops into corresponding industries that are intimately connected to the whole political and economic system. More than 12% of the entire US gross national product is devoted to health care (Burnham 1989: 357), entangling themes of health with clothing size, cardiovascular conditioning with the waistline, endurance with the body shape. Thus, however much "health" appeals to the rationality of self-preservation and offers the incentives of longevity and lowered risk of disease, messages of "health" are strongly entwined with the consumer culture idealizing appearance and the youthful body.

Connected to commodification is the process of reification, where images of abstracted body parts are styled and endowed with a life of their own, so that desirable social relationships — successful parenthood, intimate partnership, etc. — are positively influenced by purchase of the advertised objects. Reification refers to the trick through which relationships are restructured by commodities to seem "natural". Lace is merely a type of material, but is reified or coded to suggest femininity and sensuousness. What happens when a man wears lace? The seeming naturalness of the association of lace with femininity ignores the learned knowledge and the production values that have constructed the arbitrary relationship in the first place. Coloring hair to cover grey, while making sure it looks "natural," ignores other social relationships: the valuing of youth over maturity, the economic structure that results, the financial ability and desire of individuals to purchase the color, and the entire infra-structure dependent upon a person, male or female, believing in the need to transform their look.

The commodified and reified body becomes the body beautiful and is geared to the narcissistic of personal health, happiness, social success, and social acceptability. Mike Featherstone, in the article in this section titled "The Body in Consumer Culture", explores the details and theoretical underpinnings of general consumer lifestyles and bodily presentation. He suggests that attractive bodies, both male and female, are portrayed as living at the level of sheer appearance. At this level, social power is translated into economic power, with "correct" purchases displayed through focused accentuation of idealized body parts. Bodies in their natural state are interpreted by advertising as flawed body parts, exposed for the consumer industry to transform through individual efforts and self-maintenance. The time and money needed to restructure one's body into the commodified ideal ultimately reflects and can affect a person's social locations. [...]

1. Female Commodified Bodies and Commodity Feminism

Advertisements traditionally have structured a woman's view of herself from a man's (real or absent) perspective. This type of advertising is evident as early as a 1920s ad for Pompeian Night Cream. In the text of the ad, two women, one a spokesperson of the night cream, have an intimate discussion about husband and wife relationships. The other is a worried wife afraid she is losing her husband's affection. In the words of the night cream advocate, the advertisement states:

> From an unusually attractive woman my friend had developed into a chronic complainer — and it offended even *me* to see the way she appeared in the mornings at the breakfast table... So after one of her confidences I said,
>
> "Now, frankly, my dear, I believe your husband is interested in another woman. *He is interested in the woman you used to be.*" I emphasized the necessity of taking care of her complexion. I told her how bad hers looked, and how it ruined her beauty. And I was glad to tell her what almost magical results she could get by using Pompeian Night Cream.
>
> (Emphasis in original.)

The spokesperson for Pompeian Night Cream does not take the complaints of her friend/wife as real, but seeing her friend through the husband's eyes, invalidates her complaints and ignores her position and voice. Why the friend/wife is complaining is not the issue. The problem is constructed as threefold: the ability to keep the man's attention; to be worthy of his gaze; and the competition between women for the man's attention. The solution to "the problem" is a commodity: Pompeian Night Cream will keep her attractive to her man. Women are nor "naturally" acceptable, but must work at changing themselves in order to be available, receptive, and attractive to men.

Robert Goldman (1992) suggests the term "commodity feminism" to describe how the political discourse inherent in feminism has, in the 1990s, been turned into commodity style and product to be purchased. Advertisements for women today suggest that emancipation is attainable through the consumption of a product. Within this conceptualization, the female body is reframed as the location of freedom and sexual pleasure through voluntarily, knowingly, and self-reflectively becoming an object of the male gaze. In an advertisement for Triumph undergarments, a woman stands viewing her body in a full-length mirror. Her arms are over her head, holding her full head of hair, as she poses in her black bra, underwear, garter belt, and black nylons. The caption says, "I wear it. He pays attention. It's a control thing."

This advertisement demonstrates how women are now being portrayed as choosing to be sexual objects because it suits their liberated interests. Power imbalances are redressed in terms of commodity consumption, in this case, in terms of underwear and personal appearance choices. Freedom and choice are conjoined with images of sexuality and commodities. Traditionally, the idealized female slim figure allows a woman to be available to a man's attention. In this ad, she is empowered by and takes control through a traditionally commodified feminine form. Femininity as defined by the commodity leads to the control of a man. The male gaze is absent, but the style of performance is suggestive of his future perspective, internalized as part of the woman's enjoyment of herself. She actually increases her power through her ability to make herself an object, to make herself available to his gaze. Feminism is no longer focused on equal treatment or opportunity, but becomes a whole commodity consumption lifestyle displayed through the female body.

To say continually competitive, advertisers adapted feminist mandates and its rejection of ads that continuously positioned women as envying the body or the look conveyed by model images. Today's advertisements continue to use the male gaze, but are also now combining the ideals of ultrafeminine romance with an ahistoric and fictional portrayal of independence. So, while current ads still continue to address women as malleable surfaces and as resolving problems through the purchase of commodities, those commodities are positioned to exhibit tenets of feminism. These new ads juxtapose and connect the unconventional with the conventional, frequently representing women taking control and power over their lives and relationships through a commodity that determines their attractiveness to men. Advertisers may be addressing women in terms of new gender roles embracing newfound "freedoms" and life chances, but those new roles are still being structured on the same old scenarios for gaining power — using the body and appearance to simulate and stimulate desire. Through mastering the currency of "the look" whether for an assumed self-pleasure or self-determination, women are shown to acquire power over men. The commodification of different body parts is endorsed as the route to control, power, success, and strength through being attractive. Susan Bordo, titled "Material Girl" examines in depth the importance of gendered, classed, and racialized body parts as features of modern advertising. She explores how the ideals of advertising have come to shape people's experience of their bodies. The power of commodified images is shown to even structure resistance strategies to the power of advertising. Bordo comes to question Madonna's assertions of independence and resistance through her transformed appearances and constructions of "the look."

(Excerpted from J. R. Johnston: "Social Bodies" in *The American Body in Context: An Anthology*, Edited by Jessica R. Johnston, Scholarly Resources Inc., 2001.)

References

Burnham, J. The Quest for Health as the History of Modernization. *Reviews in American History*, 1989,17.

Goldman, R. *Reading Ads Socially*. New York: Routledge, 1992.

Williams, R. *Communications*. Harmondsworth: Penguin, 1968.

Questions

1. How do you understand the "structures of meaning" as mentioned by Williamson?
2. What is the use of such meanings? How do you explain "commodification"?
3. How do you understand "reification" of the human body?
4. What is "commodity feminism" mentioned by Robert Goldman? Can you give any examples?
5. In the ad with the caption "I wear it. He pays attention. It's a control thing." how do you understand the meaning of "control". Who is actually in control?
6. Can you collect some images of Madonna and illustrate "commodity feminism"?

Part II Critiquing and Resisting Gendered Body

Passage 4

Body and Power

The Following is an extract from an Interview given to Michel Foucault:

Is there a fantasy body corresponding to different types of institution?

I believe the great fantasy is the idea of a social body constituted by the universality of wills. Now the phenomenon of the social body is the effect not of a consensus but of the materiality of power operating on the bodies of individuals.

The 18th century is usually seen under the aspect of liberation. You describe it as the period when a network of forms of control (*quadrillage*) is set in place. Is the liberation possible without the *quadrillarge* ?

As always with relations of power, one is faced with complex phenomena which don't obey the Hegelian form of the dialectic. Mastery and awareness of one's own body can be acquired only through the effect of an investment of power in the body: gymnastics, exercises, muscle-building, nudism, glorification of the body beautiful. All of this belongs to the pathway leading to the desire of one's own body, by way of the insistent, persistent, meticulous work of power on the bodies of the children or soldiers, the healthy bodies. But once power produces this effect, there inevitably emerge the responding claims and affirmations, those of one's own body against power, of health against the economic system, of pleasure against the moral norms of sexuality, marriage, decency. Suddenly, what had made power strong becomes used to attack it. Power, after investing itself in the body, finds itself exposed to a counterattack in that same body. Do you recall the panic of the institutions of the social body, the doctor and politicians, at the idea of non-legalised cohabitation (*l'union libre*) or free abortions? But the impression that power weakens and vacillates here is in fact mistaken; power can retreat here, re-organize its forces, invest itself elsewhere [...] and so the battle continues.

Would this account for the much-discussed "recuperation" of the body through pornography and advertising?

I don't agree at all with the talk about "recuperation". What taking place is the usual strategic development of a struggle. Let's take a précise example, that of autoeroticism. The restrictions on masturbation hardly start in Europe until the 18th century. Suddenly, a panic-theme appears: an appalling sickness develops in the Western world. Children masturbate. Via the medium of families, though not at their initiative, a system of control of sexuality, an objectivisation of sexuality allied to corporal persecution, is established over the bodies of children. But sexuality, through thus becoming an object of analysis and concern, surveillance and control, engenders at the same time an intensification of each individual's desire, for, in and over his body.

The body thus became the issue of a conflict between parents and children, the child and the instances of control. The revolt of the sexual body is the reverse effect of this encroachment. What is the response on the side of power ? An economic and (perhaps also ideological) exploitation of eroticization, from sun-tan products to pornographic films. Responding precisely to the revolt of the body, we find a new mode of investment which presents itself no longer in the form of control by repression but that of control stimulation. "Get undressed — but be slim, good-looking, tanned!" For each move by one adversary, there is an answering one by the other. [...]

(Extracted from Michel Foucault, "Body/Power", in *Power/Knowledge: Selected Interviews and Other Writings 1972-1977*, Brighton & Sussex: Harvester Press, 1980.)

Questions

1. What is Foucault's view of power and body?
2. Does Foucault confirm the resistance to the power upon the body?
3. "Power, after investing itself in the body, finds itself exposed to a counterattack in that same body". What does it mean?
4. By the advertising message "Get undressed — but be slim, good-looking, tanned!", what does Foucault mean in terms of power and body?

Passage 5

Power, Knowledge, Body

For Foucault, modern power (as opposed to sovereign power) is non-authoritarian, non-conspiratorial, and indeed non-orchestrated; yet it none the less produces and normalises bodies to serve prevailing relations of dominance and subordination. The key "moments" of this conception (as Foucault initially theorized it and which I will now attempt to characterize) are found in "The eye of power" (1977), *Discipline and Punish* (1979), and *The History of Sexuality, Vol. I* (1980); later revisions concerning resistance are discussed in "The subject and power" (1983). Understanding how modern power operates requires , according to Foucault: first, that we cease to imagine "power" as the possession of individuals or groups — as something people "have" — and instead as dynamic or network of non-centralised forces. Secondly, we recognise that these forces are not random or haphazard, but configure to assume particular historical forms (for example, mechanisation and later scientisation of "man"). The dominance of those forms is achieved, however, not from magisterial degree or design "from above" but through multiple "processes, of different origin and scattered location", regulating the most intimate and minute elements of the construction of space, time, desire, embodiment (Foucault 1979:138). Thirdly, (and this element became central to later feminist appropriations of Foucault) prevailing forms of selfhood and subjectivity are maintained not through physical restraint and coercion, but thorough individual self-surveillance and self-correction to norms. Thus, as Foucault writes,

> There is no need for arms, physical violence, material constraints. Just a gaze. An inspecting gaze, a gaze which each individual under its weight will end by interiorizing to the point that he is his own overseer, each individual thus exercising this surveillance over, and against himself.
>
> (Foucault, 1977:155)

I would also argue [...] that this "impersonal" conception of power does not entail that there are no dominant positions, social structures or ideologies emerging from the play of forces; the fact that power is not held by anyone does not entail that it is equally held by all. It is "held" by no one; but people and groups are positioned differently within it. No one may control the rules of the game. But not all players on the field are equal. [...]

Such a model seemed to many of us particularly useful to the analysis of male dominance and female subordination, so much of which, in a modern western context, is reproduced "voluntarily", through self-normalization to everyday habits of masculinity and femininity. In my own work, Foucault's ideas were extremely helpful both to my analysis of the contemporary disciplines of diet and exercise (1990a) and to my understanding of eating disorders as arising out of and reproducing normative feminine practices of our culture. There are practices which train the female body in docility and obedience to cultural demands while at the same time being *experienced* in terms of "power" and "control" (Bordo 1985, 1990a).

(Excerpted from Susan Bordo's "Feminism, Foucault and the Politics of the Body", in *Feminist Theory and The Body: A Reader*, Edited by Janet Price & Margrit Shildrick, New York: Routledge, 1999.)

References

Foucault, M. "The Eye of Power", in C. Gordon (Ed. and Trans.), *Power/Knowledge*, New York: Pantheon, 1877.

Foucault, M. *Discipline and Punish*. New York: Vintage, 1979.

Foucault, M. *The History of Sexuality, Vol. I: An Introduction*, New York: Vintage, 1980.

Foucault, M. "The Subject and Power", L. Sawyer (Trans.), in *Michel Foucault: Beyond Structuralism and Hermeneutics*, Edited by H. L. Dreyfus and P. Rabinow. Chicago: University of Chicago Press, 1983.

Questions

1. How should modern power be interpreted?
2. What is the effect of the "gaze", upon the human body?
3. How do you explain the emergence of eating disorders, according to the author?

Passage 6

From Victims to Agents

Stereotypical representation of women has been fiercely attacked by these feminists for its construction of femininity to enslave women. But it seems that it is too totalistic to treat women merely as victims and objects of patriarchal culture, especially at the time thirty years after the feminist movement. [...] Therefore, a new awareness of women as agents possessing power should be developed and a new consciousness of women themselves as with self-worth, ability, and intelligence should also be cultivated among women, so that they could give up their passive mentality and be actively engaged in the struggle for freedom and autonomy. [...]

Judith Butler modifies her theory of gender performativity as proposed in *Gender Trouble* (1990) by putting forward a new one: the theory of gender as citation. She realizes that in the old theory of performativity, the over-emphasis of women as a cultural construction denies the agency and power of women, postulating them in a closure as passive objects in patriarchal culture. In this case, the destabilization of gender identity and sexual difference would be impossible. Hence, in *Bodies That Matter* (1993), Butler construes "performativity as citationality" (1993:12) instead of the "making do" in J. L. Austin's theory. [...] In other words, regarding the discourse of femininity in stereotypical representation in relation to the formation of women's gender identity, there exists a process of citation or materialization that promises more than one consequences. On the one hand, the appropriation of the constraining norms of sexual discourse will result in the realization of identification or a "feminine" body inscribed by the law. On the other hand, the rejection of the law or failure in materialization will result in the "abjects" or the "abnormal body". However, both rejection and reification of the law testify the agency of women in the formation of identity, which is quite contrary to the view of women as mere objects inscribed by representation. By the agency of women in gender formation, multiple bodies including the illegitimate ones are possible to appear, and the destabilization of gender identity could be realized. [...]

Contemporary feminists are aware of the power of women and therefore attempt to reject the view of women as passive objects of patriarchal culture. Looking beyond power domination, they have started to aspire for power and have observed/created new tendencies in representing the meaning of women. As Betty Friedan says, "I am sick of women wallowing in the victim state. We have empowered ourselves" (in Bordo 1997:34-35). On the other hand, postmodern consumption has also brought about opportunities of "difference" in representation: women have started to be portrayed as different and powerful. Robert Goldman (1992) discovered pluralism in the representation of female images in advertising. Susan Bordo shows the diverse bodies of "beauty" called "commercial diversity" (1997:6). The meaning of women is characterized by dialogism and ambivalence. Angela McRobbie (1994) describes this way of representation as the "changing modes of femininity" in postmodern consumer society — "judging from the evidence of the market research conducted by the new magazine it seems that girls have changed. They do not want to be represented in a humiliating way. They are not dependent on boys for their own sense of identity" (McRobbie, 1994: 164). They even resist the passive stereotypes of femininity in magazines when they "exert some power in the marketplace" (1994: 165) as they become consumers of representation. So there is the "fluidity" (1994:164) or "less rigidity" (1994:166) of the conception of femininity in representation, although "it is still predicated round the pursuit of identity (in beauty), the achievement of success (through fashion consumption) and search for some harmony or stability (through happiness)" (1994:166). In fact, McRobbie (1994: 166) describes in detail new meanings of women represented in the magazine *Just Seventeen*,

> There is more of the self in this new vocabulary of femininity, much more self-esteem, more autonomy, but still the pressure to adhere to the perfect body image as a prerequisite for the success in love which is equated with happiness. However, even here prettiness has given way to strikingness. Models are chosen from the world of real readers; they are no longer all excessively tall and exceptionally thin. There are black, mixed race and Asian models appearing on the front covers as well as on the fashion and beauty pages. There is also a redefinition of the feminine self. It can be endlessly constructed, reconstructed and customized. No longer lavishing attention on the male partner, the girl is free to lavish attention on herself and she is helped in this task by the world of consumer goods at her disposal. In love, the new female subject can expect to be treated like an equal or else feel quite entitled to "dump him".

So there appear female images other than the conventional stereotypical representation, and the mode of femininity is changing due to the consumption of identities in the marketplace. In the new language of femininity, values of "self-esteem", "autonomy" and "success" are more treasured than the identity as the male-desired "beautiful" body. To some extent, the "beauty myth" can become real myth, when it becomes women's means of self-empowering, and their sense of taking control in the male-dominated society where they aspire and strive for success. In this case, the meaning of femininity is related to women's rising power, as it is subject to their own reconstruction through consumption. This redefinition of women or the "new modes of femininity" indicates that women are not merely the objects of patriarchal culture but they are also able to change the meaning of themselves. Because of their power, the meaning of women is not fixed but is subject to change. In a word, women have started to change from their status of being cultural objects to that of social agents — they are on the way of "becoming".

(Excerpted from Shaoyan Ding: *The Construction of Meaning: A Cultural Study of Female Representation in American Magazine Advertising*, Sun Yat-sen University Press, 2007)

References

Bordo, S. *Twilight Zones: The Hidden Life of Cultural Images from Plato to O. J.* Berkeley, L. A. & London: University of California Press, 1997.

Butler, J. *Gender Trouble: Feminism and the Subversion of Identity*. New York & London: Routledge, 1990.

Butler, J. *Bodies That Matter: The Discursive Limits of Sex*. New York & London: Routledge, 1993.

Goldman, R. *Reading Ads Socially*. London & New York: Routledge, 1992.

McRobbie, A. *Postmodernism and Popular Culture*. London & New York: Routledge, 1994.

Questions

1. Can we hold it as truth that women are only victims of patriarchal culture? Why?

2. Why does Judith Butler rewrite her theory of gender identity?
3. What is Butler's view of gender identity as proposed in *Gender Trouble*? What is the significance of this view?
4. What is her new view of gender identity as proposed in *Bodies That Matter* ? How is it different from the previous one? What is the significance of this new view in relation to feminist politics?
5. Can Butler's new proposition be supported by feminist critics of advertising?
6. What does Mc'Robbie say about the meaning of Women's "Self" in studying *Just Seventeen* ? How is it related to Butler's proposition of gender identity?

Chapter 3 Representing the Racial Other

Introduction

American advertising has been stamped with racist ideology as the minority groups such as African Americans have often been represented in stereotypes due to their subordinate position in American society. And stereotypical representation of African Americans has been one of the critical issues in cultural criticism in the United States. Therefore in this chapter, stereotypes of African Americans in advertising will be examined first in order to critique the white supremacist production of the myth of black body and the identity of blackness.

Secondly, in terms of international relations, foreign countries and foreigners to the U. S. are also represented as the Other to the country. The second part of this chapter will be devoted to the investigation of this realm by examining the stereotypical representation of American foreigners and foreign land in American advertising. The notion of colonial gaze will be introduced to approach the visual representation of foreign people and foreign land. Furthermore, excerpts from Mary Louise Pratt's *Imperial Eyes* (1992) is used to understand the ideological meaning of the "wild", "exotic", "picturesque", foreign land under the colonial gaze.

Part I The Stereotyped Black Body

Passage 1

Stereotypes of African Americans in the United States

The representation of African Americans in advertising has been a topic of cultural concern in the United States. Studies show that the depictions of African Americans are displayed "against a larger background of whiteness" (O'Barr, 107). "When seen as a stream of images spanning the century, African Americans stand out as different, as divergent, and as other" (O'Barr, 107). In other words, the visual representation in advertising "has historically functioned and is currently operating to maintain a system of white supremacy"① "through a repetitive display of cultural norms and values which eventually become seen as simple 'truth'" (Ross, 1996, xix).

As a matter of fact, advertising has continually portrayed blacks in biased stereotypical images from the turn of the 20th century to the present. In the book *Aunt Jemima, Uncle Ben, and Ratus: Blacks in Advertising, Yesterday, Today, and Tomorrow* (Kern-Foxworth, 1994), the author shows that beginning with slave advertisements, slavery actually led naturally to the stereotypes found in early advertisements. Then, from the end of the slave era to the culmination of the Civil Rights movement, advertising portrayed Blacks as Aunt Jemimas, Uncle Bens, and Ratus, the portrayals of which have immense negative psychological

---

① This is quoted from B. Hawkins' article "The White Supremacy Continuum of Images of Black Men" in *Journal of African American Studies*, Vol. 3, No. 7, 7-18. Dol: 10. 1007/BF02902935. Located at Website: http://www. springerlink. com/content/h8k2704070432043/.

impacts upon the mind of African Americans and the American society. The advent of the Civil Rights movement brought about the voiced opposition to and then the elimination of such advertising. In contemporary advertising, as O'Barr (199) points, the Civil Rights movement brought about many changes in American society, including economic changes that resulted in the increasing purchasing power of African Americans in the market place. African Americans are redefined by the media as the potential, emergent market, advertisements are made for them as the intended audience and to target at them as the perspective consumers. Thus, specialized advertisements promoting goods and services to African-American audiences proliferated in magazines, on television and on neighborhood Billboards. And in promoting consumption, the codes of African Americans in advertising have to be different from those in the previous representations.

In terms of the signs of African Americans in advertising, African Americans were often are associated with images of watermelons, bananas, alligators, etc., depicted as figures in inferior or service positions, though "nowadays they can sometimes be found in positions that are even higher in status than those occupied by white people who appear in the same advertisement" (O'Barr, 108). And in contemporary advertising, African Americans are not often depicted as service positions, but more frequently shown as sports figures or athletic superstars: basketball and tennis players or jazz musicians.

In spite of the changes in ad representation of African Americans, the racist/white supremacist representation continue, with the "social construction of images for black men" which has "caused them to be feared by the public or used for mass entertainment for them"①.

---

① This is quoted from B. Hawkins' article "The White Supremacy Continuum of Images of Black Men" in *Journal of African American Studies*, Vol. 3, No. 7, 8. Dol: 10. 1007/BF02902935. Located at Website: http://www. springerlink. com/content/h8k2704070432043/.

According to Hawkins, if slavery is the system of control over the black body, representing negative images of black men within white supremacist thinking is the ideological hegemony to dominate the black body. Two dominant images of African American men in advertising are the sambo image and the brutal nigger image. The sambo image represents a domesticated, a childish, happy, contented slave who knows his place and thus is subservient and highly dependent on his master, and is no threat to white supremacy (Pieterse, 1992). Thus it seems to be embraceable or palatable by the public. But as the brutal nigger image, an untamed sambo, a bestial (or beast-like in physicality), demon-like savage controlled by his violent sexual impulses (Pierterse, 1992) poses a threat to the society and the system, it is unembraceable by the public. The two images serve different purposes. The sambo image of a black man often appear in advertisements, such as "Uncle Ben's Rice", "Uncle Remus Syrup", or male image in the ad for the Cream of Wheat Nabisco products. The brutal nigger image first appeared in the D. W. Griffith's film *Birth of a Nation* (1915) as the sexual violator of white women and political ravagers, and is often present in films (e. g. blacks as criminals) and advertising. The sambo/coon and the brutal nigger images "represent two points on the continuum of white supremacy by which the representation of black men are placed and can shift from the domesticated or demonized idea depending on the need of the system"①.

References

Kern-Foxworth, M. *Aunt Jemima, Uncle Ben, and Rastus: Blacks in*

① This is quoted from B. Hawkins' article "The White Supremacy Continuum of Images of Black Men" in *Journal of African American Studies*, Vol. 3, No. 7, 10. DoI: 10. 1007/BF02902935. Located at Website: http://www. springerlink. com/content/h8k2704070432043/.

Advertising, Yesterday, Today, and Tomorrow. Westport, CT: Praeger, 1994.

O'Barr, W. *Culture and the Ad: Exploring Otherness in the World of Advertising*. Westview Press, 1994.

Ross, K. *Black and White Media: Black Images in Popular Film and Television*. Cambridge, MA: Polity Press, 1996.

Pieterse, J. N. *White on Black: Images of Africa and Blacks in Western Popular Culture*. New Haven: Yale University Press, 1992.

Questions

1. Historically, how are African Americans represented in American advertising? Why are they represented as such?
2. How are African Americans represented in contemporary advertising? Why?
3. How do you understand/critique the stereotypical representation of African Americans in American advertising?

Passage 2

Advertising to the Black Audience

Television, of course, wasn't the only media to fail in representing the realities of Black middle-class life, converging around stereotypes to dismiss a whole segment of high-achieving African American families. A look back through advertising archives reveals nearly a hundred years of marketers missing the mark. In fact, looking back on the advertisements that featured images of Blacks in the early part of the twentieth century is not just offensive — it is downright cringe-worthy.

Though ads featuring Blacks in the 1960s increased in number, "the manner in which they were portrayed tended to confirm and perpetuate racial stereotypes." Later, however, "improvements" in the occupational status of Black models in magazine ads were evident. There was an increase in the use of Black models between 1967 and 1974, but they "tended to advertise personal items, such as hair products, rather than nonpersonal products, such as automobiles".

However, the 1960s and 1970s did bring some small breakthroughs in the way Blacks were represented in media. The young and growing generation of middle-class Blacks was taken seriously by advertisers like never before. Levi's, Lee, and J. C. Penney competed to dress the rising Black middle-class. Greyhound appealed to Black travelers with an ad featuring two napping children riding together side-by-side — a young, White boy dressed as an Indian and a Black boy dressed as a cowboy. Atlantic City advertised its "boardwalk bonanza" with print ads showcasing a young Black couple building sand castles on its beach. Armstrong Tires targeted this audience with a rather strange ad: a photo of a young Black woman posed seductively beside a tire under the headline "the tire for lovers".

Not all advertising to this audience was a step in the right direction, of course. Johnnie Walker Red, Hiram Walker bourbon, and Martini and Rossi Vermouth were among the legal beverage ads that featured Black faces enjoying their products, as did ads for Viceroy, Tareyton, and Kent cigarettes — and it is the ads for these kinds of adult products around which controversy still swirls. In 1991 a report from the Stanford Center for Research in Disease Prevention did an analysis of billboard placement in neighborhoods in San Francisco, California. What they found was that "across all billboard advertising of products and services, tobacco (19%) and alcohol (17%) were most heavily advertised." Furthermore, "Black neighborhoods had the highest rate of billboards per 1000 population," and "Black neighborhoods were proportionately more likely than other neighborhoods to have billboards advertising menthol cigarettes and malt liquor."

Twelve years later, these industries were still disproportionately targeting the Black audience. A 2003 study by Georgetown University's Center on Alcohol Marketing and Youth found that, of the $333 million in advertising placed by the nation's alcohol industry that year, "Blacks from 12 to 20 years old saw 77% more of these ads [...] than their non-Black peers did."

It was obvious the industry was "directly targeting Black kids," according to the Reverend Jesse Brown, executive director of the National Association of African Americans for Positive Imagery. "African American kids tend to be trendsetters in what they buy, so the industry thinks if it can get more African American kids to buy, it can also get their White counterparts to buy."

It's not merely inappropriate placement, or overplacement, of ads that expose young Blacks to adult or unhealthy products that remains a disappointingly contemporary issue. But let us suggest that some of the lingering problems with the limited or misrepresentative images of African Americans in creative has to do with the historic lack of Blacks in the executive offices of advertising agencies. Through the decades, though Blacks were targeted by advertisers, and there were some Black faces in print and television ads, the people who created those ads were rarely themselves Black. In fact, there was a time when it was so rare to find an African American in an executive position in an advertising agency that the 1970 movie *Putney Swope* — tagged as "the truth and soul movie"— featured a comedic storyline about an advertising firm that accidentally voted in the Black partner as the new head of the company. In real life, of course, things weren't quite that comical. The late Vince Cullers of Chicago launched the first Black advertising agency in 1956, while Luis D?az Albertini founded the first Latino shop, Spanish Advertising and Marketing Services, in 1962 to attempt to both appeal to these minority segments as well as improve the images that represented them in the mass media. Jason Chambers, a professor of advertising at the University of Illinois, tells the inside story of the history of Blacks in the ad business in his book, *Madison Avenue and the Color Line: African Americans in the Advertising Industry*. He writes that Blacks in advertising in the early days of the 1960s and 1970s saw themselves as having a "dual responsibility" to their clients to sell products to the Black community while working to change its often negative image. "Their lowly status in advertisements confirmed their economic disenfranchisement, just as violence and Jim Crow laws confirmed their political disenfranchisement," Chambers wrote, but "getting to that point [...] first required getting white-owned companies to recognize the black consumer market."

Getting companies to recognize the underserved and generally untapped Black market — especially the AAA market — is our ongoing challenge. And companies like Lagrant Communications, Muse Communications, and UniWorld help marketers reach multicultural consumers. These are important moves forward as we estimate that of total ad spending in the United States, less than 4 percent is directed at any level of minority consumer.

Still, for every Allstate ad featuring a Dennis Haysbert (the actor perhaps best-known for portraying America's first Black president on the television show 24), there are two or more that feature African Americans in stereotypical (i. e., dancing or playing sports) or even subservient roles. In one strikingly unfortunate image, Intel advertised its Core 2 Duo Desktop Processor with a photo of six athletic Black men in cubicles bowing down to one White man who has arms cockily crossed and a smug smile on his face. This image is under the headline, "Multiply computing performance and maximize the power of your employees." We wonder if Intel gave a thought to the evocation of subservience in this ad — or to how that image might play with African

American consumers.

It is ads like this one that can make us appreciate Gucci's marketing campaign with Rihanna. However misguided these ads are as an attempt to attract the AAA segment, they do feature the image of a beautiful, strong, and empowered Black woman.

(Excerpted from Leonard E. Burnett, Jr. and Andrea Hoffman: *Black Is the New Green*, Palgrave Macmillan, a Division of Macmillan Publishers Limited.)

Questions

1. How are black people represented in American advertising in 1960s and 1970s?
2. Did the advertising images in American advertising in 1960s and 1970s truly represent life of Black people?
3. What is the new strategy to target at African American people?
4. What are the reasons for the lingering existence of stereotypes of Black people?

Further Reading: Decoding African American Images in Advertisements

The appendix of this book (p. 129) consists a number of trade cards, art-crafts and advertisements showing black images. Please "read" them and sort out the stereotypes exploited to represent African Americans. You may read Passages 1&2 for reference.

Part II Critiquing Stereotypes of African Americans

Passage 3

Colonial Discourse and the Construction of the Other

An important feature of colonial discourse is its dependence on the concept of "fixity" in the ideological construction of Other. Fixity, as the sign of cultural/historical/racial difference in the discourse of colonialism, is a paradoxical mode of representation: it connotes rigidity and an unchanging order as well as disorder, degeneracy and daemonic repetition. Likewise, the stereotype, which is its major discursive strategy, is a form of knowledge and identification that vacillates between what is always "in place", already known, and something that must be anxiously repeated — as if the essential duplicity of the Asiatic or bestial sexual license of the African that needs no proof, can never, in discourse, be proved. It is this process of ambivalence, central to the stereotype, that my essay explores as it constructs a theory of colonial discourse (in Evans & Hall, Eds. 2002:370).

(Colonial discourse) is an apparatus that turns on the recognition and disavowal of racial/cultural/historical differences. Its predominant strategic function is the creation of a space for a "subject peoples" through the production of knowledges in terms of which surveillance is exercised and a complex form of pleasure/unpleasure is incited. Its seeks authorisation for its strategies by the production of knowledges of coloniser and the colonised which are stereotypical but antithetically evaluated. The objective of colonial discourse is to construe the colonised as a population of degenerate types on the basis of racial origin, in order to justify conquest and to establish systems of administration and instruction. [...] Therefore, [...] colonial discourse produces the colonised as a fixed reality which is at once an "other" and yet entirely knowable and visible. It resembles a form of narrative whereby the productivity and circulation of subjects and signs are bound in a reformed and recognisable totality. It employs a system of representation, a regime of truth, that is structurally similar to Realism" (in Evans & Hall, Eds. 2002:371).

(Excerpted from Homi K. Bhabha's "The Other Question:

Stereotype and Colonial Discourse", in *Visual Culture: the Reader*, Ed. by Evans & Hall, Eds. 2002.)

Questions

1. What is the primary characteristic of stereotypes?
2. Why do stereotypes belong to "a paradoxical mode of representation"?
3. What is the function of stereotypes? How are stereotypes related to the colonial discourse?
4. How do you employ Bhabha's view of stereotypes to critique stereotypes of African Americans in the United States?

Passage 4

The Myth of Race and the Black Bestial Sexuality

Scholarship has traced the interconnections between racism and the body, showing how the body has been central to the actual construction of the concept of race. The race of a person is usually initially identified from the visible body; the lips, eyes, hair, and skin color. Yet, many bodies share these visible traits outside the narrowed category of "race." The distribution of physical characteristics is scattered across the spectrum of humanity, revealing again the arbitrary nature of classifications and categorizations. The racialized body is interpreted as visible exposing the essential relationship between a region, or a continent, or a history, collapsing these seeming distinctions into an "epidermal hierarchy" of culture and identity (Wiegman, 1995: 9). Race becomes embodied as a visual marker, translating seemingly observable physical differences, geographies, politics, and ideology into the "naturalness" of the body (Wiegman, 1995: 22).

That "naturalness" usually has an assumed foundation in biology. The eugenics movement and the study of cranial capacity at the turn of the nineteenth century, the Jensen Report of the late 1960s, and The Bell Curve in the mid-1990s are all examples of the promotion of this naturalized racial biology. This view objectifies race, dividing people into categories that combine entwined biological, sociological, and cultural types. [...] When biological and cultural explanations are juxtaposed, biological explanations tend to dominate. Race constructed as a biological category becomes "scientifically" interpreted as a neutral and natural genetic category.

In the 19th century, "scientific" measurement of the brain and skull was used to explain the differences between individuals and groups. In the 1820s, phrenology claimed a direct comparison between women and "lower races" based on their skull formation. "In short, lower races represented the 'female' type of the human species, and females the 'lower races' of gender" (Stepan 1990: 39-40). Through these measurements, the African male was aligned with "the feminine." Whether it was brain weight, cranial capacity, the facial angle, or the brain volume, an "objective" measure was found to substantiate the differences between social superiorities and inferiorities.

These types of physical and social categorizations, while being an arbitrary grouping of traits, have real consequences in people's lived experiences. "Race" cannot be abstracted from the social and political environment within which it is defined and lived. The entwined commingling of biological, historical, and cultural categorizations affects social and political stratification.

Recently, scholars have explored how these social conceptualizations of racial differences have displayed divisions similar to the mind/body split inherent in Cartesian dualism. Naturalists in the 17th century presumed man was "mind" while woman was confined to the sensuous and physical "body". These naturalists also assumed the African body, both male and female, embodied a seemingly degenerated racial sexuality. Africans were seen as sexually uninhibited "creatures" with unlimited appetites and satisfactions. And while it was accepted that women in general were lower than men, comparison of African and European female bodies revealed they were biologically different from one another. The "nonwhite" woman was thought to be endowed with an uncontrolled animalistic sexuality — a myth that justified the use of black women for slave breeding and exempted them from the possibility of being raped. By linking the body with both femininity and "animality," "women of color" entwined both sexuality and race.

The construction of difference between white men and African men was based on the perception of both the African's seemingly smaller brain capabilities along with his "perversely developed" sexuality. In patriarchal relations, men's dominance over women is the primary sign of power. White men were the defenders of white female sexuality. In the slave economy, black men were "scientifically" feminized as inferior through phrenological measurements. This feminization is represented in the bumbling black Sambo, Uncle Remus, and Jim Crow.

During reconstruction, though, the Freedman's Bureau gave the black male theoretical equality in political and economic spheres. In theory, he became part of the patriarchy — head of the household, able to enter into contractual labor agreements for the entire family, taking on the gender codes of white bourgeois ideology. Theorists suggest that this legal enfranchisement of the black male slave during Reconstruction heightened the threat to white masculine supremacy. Black males were now to enter the public arena with all the rights and privileges of men. The black man's threat to white masculine power arose from the frightening possibility of cross-race masculine sameness.

This threat of masculine sameness combines with the fear that slaves, freed from the restraining influences of slavery, were "retrogressing" toward their "natural state" of bestiality. Older slaves were susceptible to the fall, but more threatening were the young men who, born free, bad never felt the "civilizing" effects of slavery. The essential nature of the newly matured black man was seen as bestial and supported by the enforced moral behavior of slavery. The "new Negro" was reverting to a native savagery, a "reversion" that became most conspicuous in fabricated reports of black men raping white women. The black man was reduced to the body, and to the penis itself. The black freed man was "man" without mind, hyper-masculinized as the black-beast-rapist.

This hyper-masculinized construction has extended into the twentieth century in the Black Power movement. Even the *Shaft* and *Superfly* figures from the 1970s suggest images of the powerfully masculine black male. The image of black man is one of the physical prowess and a "natural athleticism," and is discussed in detail in this section by Mary G. McDonald, in "Michael Jordan's Family Values: Marketing, Meaning, and Post-Reagan America." McDonald explores how Jordan is able to counter the attributed white fears of black men, exploiting normative male values of athletic success and fatherhood. He consciously constructs his black body into a symbol of masculinity and white corporate achievement, commodifying black athleticism as freedom and economic prosperity.

(Excerpted from Jessica R. Johnston: "Social Bodies", in *The American Body in Context: An Anthology*, Ed. by Jessica R. Johnston, Scholarly Resources Inc., 2001.)

References

Stepan, N. "Race and Gender: The Role of Analogy in Science". In *the Anatomy of Racism*, Edited by D. T. Goldberg. Minneapolis: University of Minnesota Press, 1990.

Wiegman, R. *American Anatomies: Theorizing Race and Gender.*

Durham. NC: Duke University Press, 1995.

Questions

1. What is "race", according to the author? How is it defined?
2. Is the term "race" natural? How do you understand the "naturalness" of race? Is "race" a neutral, scientific measurement of genetic category?
3. Why was the African male aligned with the "feminine"? Is such equation scientific?
4. How is the mind/body split related to the definition of Africans? How come there is the myth of black degenerate sexuality? Why are non-white women linked with sexuality?
5. What is the consequence of linking black body with brute sexuality?

Passage 5

The Fact of Blackness

"Dirty nigger!" Or simply, "Look, a Negro!"

I came into the world imbued with the will to find a meaning in things, my spirit filled with the desire to attain to the source of the world and then I found that I was an object in the midst of other objects.

Sealed into that crushing objecthood, I turned beseechingly to others. Their attention was a liberation, running over my body suddenly abraded into nonbeing, endowing me once more with an agility that I had thought lost, and by taking me out of the world, restoring me to it. But just as I reached the other side, I stumbled, and the movements, the attitudes, the glances of the other fixed me there, in the sense in which a chemical solution is fixed by a dye. I was indignant; I demanded an explanation. Nothing happened. I burst apart. Now the fragments have been put together again by another self.

As long as the black man is among his own, he will have no occasion, except in minor internal conflicts, to experience his being through others. There is of course the moment of "being for others", of which Hegel speaks, but every ontology is made unattainable in a colonized and civilized society. It would seem that this fact has not been given sufficient attention by those who have discussed the question. In the *Weltanschauung* of a colonized people there is an impurity, a flaw that outlaws any ontological explanation. Someone may object that this is the case with every individual, but such an objection merely conceals a basic problem. Ontology — one it is finally admitted as leaving existence by the wayside — does not permit us to understand the being of the black man. For not only must the black man be black; he must be black in relation to the white man. [...] The black man has no ontological resistance in the eyes of the white man. Overnight the Negro has been given two frames of reference within which he has had to place himself. His metaphysics, or, less pretentiously, his customs and the sources on which they were based, were wiped out because they were in conflict with a civilization that he did not know and that imposed itself on him.

"Look, a Negro!" It was an external stimulus that flicked over me as I passed by. I made a tight smile.

"Look, a Negro!" It was true. It amused me.

"Look, a Negro!" The circle was drawing a bit tighter. I made no secret of my amusement.

"Mama, see the Negro! I'm frightened!" Frightened! Frightened! Now they were beginning to be afraid of me. I made up my mind to laugh myself to tears, but laughter had become impossible.

I could no longer laugh, because I already knew that there were legends, stories, history, and above all *historicity*, which I had learned about from Jaspers. Then, assailed at various points, the corporeal schema crumbled, its place taken by a racial epidermal schema. In the train it was no longer a question of being aware of my body in the third person but in a triple person. In the train I was given not one but two, three places. I had already stopped being amused. It was not that I was finding febrile coordinates in the world. I existed triply: I occupied space. I moved towards the other — and the evanescent other, hostile but not opaque, transparent, not there, disappeared. Nausea. [...]

I was responsible at the same time for my body, for my race, for my ancestors. I subjected myself to an objective examination, I discovered my blackness, my ethnic characteristics; and I was battered down by tom-toms, cannibalism, intellectual deficiency, fetishism, racial defects, slave-ships, and above all else, above all: "Sho 'good eatin'."

On that day, completely dislocated, unable to be abroad with the other, the white man, who unmercifully imprisoned me, I took myself far off from my own presence, far indeed, and made myself an object. What else could it be for me but an amputation, an excision, a hemorrhage that spattered my whole body with black blood? But I did not want this revision, this thematization. All I wanted was to be a man among other men. I wanted to come lithe and young into a world that was ours and to help to build it together.

"Look at the nigger! [...] Mama, a Negro! [...] Hell, he's getting mad. [...] Take no notice, sir, he does not know that you are as civilized as we. [...]"

My body was given back to me sprawled out, distorted, recolored, clad in mourning in that whit winter day. The Negro is an animal, the Negro is bad, the Negro is mean, the Negro is ugly; look, a nigger, it's cold, the nigger is shivering, the nigger is shivering because he is cold, the little boy is trembling because he is afraid of the nigger, the nigger is shivering with cold, that cold that goes through your bones, the handsome little boy is trembling because he thinks that the nigger is quivering with rage, the little white boy throws himself into his mother's arms: Mama, the nigger's going to eat me up.

All round me the white man, above the sky tears at its navel, the earth rasps under my feet, and there is a white song, a white song. All this whiteness that burns me. [...]

(Excerpted from Fanon, Frantz. *Black Skin*, *White Masks*. New York: Grove Press, 1986:109-139.)

Questions

1. Why does Fanon say that he is an "object"?
2. What are Blacks like in Whites' eyes? Are they defined based on the understanding of Black people's culture? Is there any ontological understanding of Black people?
3. How do you describe the effect of "blackness" upon Blacks' mind?

Part III Otherizing Foreigners and Foreign Land

Passage 6

Feminizing the Other and the Colonial Gaze in American Advertising

Americans has never hesitated to represent foreigners in stereotypes — images of foreigners viewed from American perspective, with Americans as the center of power. American advertising is saturated with the discourse of the Other and the consciousness of the privilege of the Americans, as O'Barr says in examining the stereotypical images of non-American people in a UPS ad, "(American advertisements) convey in their secondary discourse an ideology about the relations of Americans and foreigners that is repeated elsewhere in other advertisements. Such recurrent patterns establish and continually reinforce ideas about social relationships and intercultural exchanges. They describe international relations and the locus of world power. At the core of this discourse are lessons about dominance and hierarchy, subordination and inequality. In their own time and place, these messages about otherness embedded within contemporary advertising no less important as a form of public instruction than were biblical teachings depicted in the etched windows of Gothic cathedrals or the paintings on cave walls in other ages" (1994: 74-75). In O'Barr's idea, in American advertising stereotypical images of foreigners not only convey and teach the knowledge of the foreigners based on American relationship to them, with Americans in power position and the foreigners as the Other. American advertising is a space for spreading American ideological values.

In O'Barr's investigation, American advertising consist of stereotypes for different people: the West and the Non-West. While the West is often presented as having history, the Non-West is often described as having traditions. The reason is that "Western history is venerated and used to explain America's origins; Non-Western traditions are exotic yet interesting. Advertisements that depict Europe often show a different kind foreigner from those that depict Caribbean or Asia. These are not absolute differences that occur in every depiction but patterns established through frequent repetition" (O'Barr, 1994: 75). One important characteristic of contemporary American advertising is the feminine metaphor for otherness: the depiction of the Other (the West and the non-West) as feminine or child-like, which is relate to the issue of the feminine as the Other in feminist critique. It can be seen in the ads representing Europe and Asia, where female images are often appropriated for advertisements for Japanese products and Asian airlines. Besides, land in foreign countries, Asian especially, is depicted as picturesque and exotic. And the purpose of such signification is to show "the dominance over foreigners" and the submissiveness and subordination of the Other.

Secondly, this "Other" of the foreign is also subjected to the technological and imperial gaze in the visual convention.

As advertising is related to the photographic technology, which is used to record people and objects, the photographic gaze is highly meaningful in power relationship in terms of the camera/viewer/spectator and the objects/land framed in the camera. As M. Sturken and L. Cartright say (2001: 100),

> The photographic gaze thus helps to establish relationships of power. The person with the camera looks at a person, event, place, or object. The act of looking is commonly thought of as awarding more power to the person who is looking than to the person who is the object of the look. The tradition of institutional photography, in which prisoners, mental patients, and people of various ethnicities were photographed and catalogued, can be related to the traditions of visual anthropology and travel photography as well as to the tradition of painting peoples of so-called exotic locales. All function to varying degrees to represent codes of dominance and subjugation, difference and otherness.

So the gazer and the gazed at is relationship: the gaze from the seer/viewer/camera is the agent who has power over what is gazed at—the subject as subordinate. In travel photography and advertising, when the traveler is looking at the land and people of the foreign/exotic and assumes a gazer-object relationship with the local surroundings, this gaze can be termed as the colonial gaze.

The colonial gaze is ever-present in travel advertising which promotes trips to a different space by visual representation and in advertising which sell goods by associating them with the land/space of the foreign (usually the third-world countries). Here, land is usually depicted as natural, picturesque or "wild" to attract perspective tourists/consumers, mostly from the first world countries (American and European countries). Then, in magazines on travel, global geography and anthropological examination of the foreign, such as the American *National Geographic*, there tend to be tremendous signification of Otherness represented by the depictions/photos of the "wild", picturesque and often spectacular scenery of the other continents, together with the special/different ways of life of the local people. The land and people there are simply gazed at by the camera in white male hands and created as the Other to entertain American/White/European readers and tourists.

References

O'Barr, W. *Culture and the Ad: Exploring Otherness in the World of Advertising*. Westview Press, 1994.

Sturken, M. & Cartwright, L. *Practices of Looking: An Introduction to Visual Culture*. Oxford: Oxford University Press, 2001.

Questions

1. How are the West and the Non-West represented in American advertising? Can you give any specific examples (of ads) to illustrate such representation?
2. What is the icon specifically used to represent the foreign countries to America? And why?
3. What theories from Cultural Studies can be used as an effective critique of the stereotypes of Asians?
4. Have you noticed the representation of Asian Americans in the United

States? What is it like? Is the representation the same as the representation of people and land in Asian countries?

5. What is "colonial gaze"?
6. How is it related to the "male gaze"?

Passage 7

The Meaning of Colonial Gaze

How to understand the colonial gaze? How to understand the visual representation of the "wild" foreign land? The following excerpt from Mary Louise Pratt's *Imperial Eyes* (1992) will help us understand the meaning of "wildness" in the colonial gaze. Here, Pratt is commenting and critiquing Alexander von Humboldt's travel writing with the depictions of the land of South America in his eyes. Read the following paragraphs and then answer the questions.

It was through his non-specialized writings rather than his scientific treatises that Humboldt sought, and won, his broadest impact on the public imaginations of Europe and Euroamerica. [...] Travel writings in the immediate sense, these non-specialized works are also bold discursive experiments in which, as I will argue, Humboldt sought to reinvent popular imaginings of America, and through America, of the planet itself. Even as he undertook to recreate South America in connection with its new opening to Northern Europe, Humboldt sought simultaneously to reframe bourgeois subjectivity, heading off its sundering of objectivist and subjectivist strategies, science and sentiment, information and experience. Along with others of his time, he proposed to Europeans a new kind of planetary consciousness.

[...]

In point of fact, it took a highly selective reception of Humboldt's writings to reduce South America to pure nature and the iconic triad of mountains, plain, and jungle. I will be referring below to some of the other ways in which Humboldt wrote and thought about South America, notably archeological and demographic ones. But it was unquestionably the image of primal nature elaborated in his scientific works and his *Views* that became codified in the European imaginary as the new ideology of the "new continent". Why? For one thing, the ideology, like the continent, was precisely not new. 19th-century Europeans reinvented America as Nature in part because that is how 16th- and 17th-century Europeans had invented America for themselves in the first place, and for many of the same reasons. Though deeply rooted in 18th-century constructions of Nature and Man, Humboldt's seeing-man is also a self-conscious double of the first European inventors of America, Columbus, Vespucci, Raleigh, and the others. They, too, wrote America as a primal world of nature, an unclaimed and timeless space occupied by plants and creatures (some of them human), but not organized by societies and economies; a world whose only history was the one about to begin. Their writings too portrayed America in a discourse of accumulation, abundance, and innocence. Humboldt's rhapsodic invocation of a flourishing primal world echoes such writings as Columbus' famous letter to the Spanish monarchs in 1493. [...]

[...] The point is not to argue that Humboldt's representations were somehow implausible or lacking in verisimilitude. I do want to argue, however, that they were not inevitable, that their contours were conditioned by a particular historical and ideological juncture, and by particular relations of power and privilege. South America didn't *have* to be invented or reinvented as primal nature. Despite the emphasis on primal nature, in all their explorations, Humboldt and Bonpland never once stepped beyond the boundaries of the Spanish colonial infrastructure — they couldn't, for they relied entirely on the networks of villages, missions, outposts, haciendas, roadways, and colonial labor systems to sustain themselves and their project, for food, shelter, and the labor pool to guide them and transport their immense equipage. Even the canonical images of interior plains, snowcapped mountains, and dense jungles did not lie outside the history of humankind, or even the history of Euroimperialism. The inhabitants of the Venezuelan *llanos* and the Argentine pampas, however removed from colonial centers, were about to be recruited as soldiers in the wars of independence. The jungle had been penetrated by the colonial mission system, whose influence extended far beyond the microcosmic social orders of its outposts. The Andean Cordillera (Humboldt's "mountain solitudes") was also the living place for most of the inhabitants of Peru, among whom pre-Columbian life ways and colonial resistance. continued to be powerful everyday realities. Historically, it was also the great mother lode of colonial mineral wealth. [...]

[...] Every travel account has this heteroglossic dimension; its knowledge comes not just out of a traveler's sensibility and powers of observation, but out of interaction and experience usually directed and managed by "travelees", who are working from their own understandings of their world and of what the Europeans are and ought to be doing. [...]

(Excerpted from Sturken, Marita & Cartwright, Lisa. *Practices of Looking: An Introduction to Visual Culture*, 2001.)

Notes

Alexander von Humboldt and Aime Bonpland were Spanish explorers who travelled to South America in 1799 and stayed there, the New Continent, for the rest five years. Their historic journey in print represents the ideological endeavor to redefine South America.

References

Pratt, M. L. *Imperial Eyes*, London: Routledge, 1992.

Questions

1. How does the author describe Humboldt's travel writing? Is it an objective portrayal of the New Continent?
2. What is the new continent like in Humboldt and Columbus' eyes? What is the exact word used by the author to refer to the two men's views?
3. According to the author, what motivates Humboldt's representation from socio-cultural perspective?
4. In the latter half of Paragraph 3, what is the tone of voice like?
5. Based on Pratt's critique of Humboldt's depictions of South America, how do you understand the depictions of land and people in travel advertising and the *National Geographic* magazine?

Chapter 4 Marketing Youth Culture

Introduction

Today, a great deal of advertising is fashion ads, especially the ads for youth fashion, branded to target at the youth market. Such ads are very popular in magazines and on the Internet, which are influential to the personal of youth. Therefore, this chapter brings students into the world of youth fashion, with special attention to the understanding of the particular cultural meanings of fashion, branding, and the commercialization of youth culture.

While Part I concerns the definition of fashion as language/codes and aspirations of identity in relation to the social structure such as class and gender, Part II explores the nature of branding — the infusing of cultural meanings into the packaged goods to create an identity for commercial promotion. These two important notions of commercial culture pave the way for the understanding of the marketing of youth culture in Part II — the branding of commodities/clothes with elements of youth culture and creating brands as fashion for youth's consumption. Furthermore, the meaning of youth culture is also introduced in order that the whole picture of corporate marketing of youth culture can be better understood.

Part I The Meaning of Fashion

Passage 1

Fashion as a Social Code

Fashion theory is frequently punctuated with references to the "language of clothes", a phrase made popular by Alison Lurie in the early 1980s (Lurie, 1992). This phrase suggests that clothes somehow have the power of articulation, that appearances "speak". The metaphor that fashion is a language has persisted despite the obvious failure of clothing to produce the fundamental requirements of a language, namely, an explicit vocabulary, parts of speech, syntax and dialogue. Clothes do not speak to us or to one another; they do not sustain a system of meaningful exchange. Social encounters constituted by language are unscripted, flexible and unpredictable. Even if, by a generous reckoning, we allow that clothes can make "make a statement", they are not capable of nuanced exchange, While meanings proliferate through human speech, clothing remains static; while words change their meaning only slowly, the fashionability of clothing — and hence the meanings it disseminates — changes every season (Davis, 1992:7-8). To speak of the "language" of clothes is to acknowledge the persistence of this metaphor rather than to discover a conventional linguistic system embedded in materials produced by the fashion industry.

Both Hollander (1980) and Lurie (1992) employ the metaphor of clothes as a language. Lurie calls clothes and fashion accessories a "visual language" with its own grammar, syntax and vocabulary. Her analysis, which sometimes reads like parody, enunciates the exact meanings and aesthetic formations carried by certain images. The red necktie favoured by President Ronald Reagan during the early 1980s, for example, is interpreted as symbolizing virility and heterosexuality. In this instance, the ordinary necktie becomes a statement of conventionalized sexual practices. "A man's tie may also sexually symbolic", Lurie informs us, "especially if it is brightly colored of in some way unusual". In her reading, "the tieless Catholic priest is 'symbolically castrated'", and "the narrow woven cord or leather thong ties often favored by elderly American men suggest a withering or drying up of the passion" (1992:244-245).

This assumed correspondence between inner and outer spheres suggests that clothing can be used either deliberately to promote oneself to interested on-lookers, or inadvertently to betray one's inner, secret self. Dress maps on to the self, according to Lurie: "the woman in the sensible grey wool suit and the frilly pink blouse is a serious, hard-working mouse with a frivolous and feminine soul" (ibid.: 245). Clothing is a shorthand for social status. Lurie argues:

> The well-to-do can be observed to have on more clothes. The men are more likely to wear vests; the women are more apt to wear panty hose, superfluous scarves and useless little wraps. [...] On the beach, though the rich may splash into the waves in suites as skimpy as anyone else's, the moment they emerge they will make a dash for the conspicuous raw-silk beach kimono, terry swim dress or linen shirt that matches their bathing suit and restores the status quo. (ibid.:121)

Although Barthes (1985) and Lévi-Strauss (1972) retain the metaphor of a semiotic system, both recognise that fluidities and ambiguities inherent in the structure of fashionable appearance force its codes to remain open-ended. Lurie remains confident in her interpretations of colours, styles, textures and fabrics; others are more aware of the instability of meaning transmitted through these methods, which include the ways in which clothes are worn, and the body postures that different individuals adopt. This leads the semioticians of fashion to conclude that while fashions obviously speak, it is unclear what they say (Davis, 1992:6). It may be possible to posit some rules, such as that dark colours suggest formality, light colours informality, angularity masculinity, and curvilinear forms femininity, yet for every rule there will immediately appear a series of anomalies. The fact that styles in clothing change quickly — making their status and value hard to locate — supports the view that clothes are a source of unresolved ambiguity.

In his essay on American clothing, the anthropologist Marshall Sahlins (1976:179-204) adopts a structuralist perspective to argue that colour (light or dark), hue (bright or dull), texture (rough or smooth), direction (horizontal or vertical) and line (straight or curved) all serve to encode in clothes the fundamental cultural distinctions of gender, status, age, occupation, lifestyle, ethnicity, and sexuality, and they do so in ways which are largely unrecognized and unconscious. He maintains that the visuality of clothes enables them to express specific binary opposites, such as being chaste (or not), open (or not), and refined (or not). Other non-visual cues include the olfactory (such as floral perfumes which suggest modesty) and the tactile (body oils which suggest sexiness). A structuralist view of fashion assumes that stable meanings can be uncovered.

Davis (1992:91-92) argues against this position by suggesting that all consumer items — including fashionable clothes, avant-garde furniture, popular music, and objects of all kinds — have unstable meanings when they first appear on the cultural horizon. The relationship between the signifier (or word) and the signified (or thing) is arbitrary and therefore uncontrolled. Clothing items are especially ambivalent. The bra, for example, both contains and controls the breasts but also highlights them. Trousers not only conceal the male genitals but also (with the tailored fly) draw attention to them. Moreover, the meaning of consumer items is highly differentiated in terms of taste, social identity, and cultural capital. As Bourdieu (1984) has demonstrated in his empirical study of taste in French society, the function of fashion is frequently to activate these forces of differentiation. Should the relationship between the signifier and signified be weak, then the resultant "undercoding" will produce a wide range of unanticipated interpretations and the absence of reliable knowledge. In this respect, fashion is like a aesthetic code, which is expected to be supple, and immediately able to parody, undermine, and extend the boundaries of the objects to which it refers.

[...]

Even if fashion clothing is not strictly speaking a linguistic system, it is a mode of communication implicated in the expression of individual identity. Simmel argues that dress and other forms of fashion enable the modern urban dweller to balance the conflicting demands of social conformity with private desires for individuality. Fashion extrudes the ambivalences produced by a social self. This formulation of identity follows the precepts of social philosophers like George Herbert Mead and Charles Peirce, who assume that language is the essential socializing agent. For them, the self is produced through an inner dialogue. Fashionable dress can easily be inserted into such interior exchanges because it straddles the segregated spheres of private and public. Davis considers fashion capable of reflecting the modern, phenomenological self: "dress, then, comes easily to serve as a kind of visual metaphor for identity and, as pertains in particular to the open societies of the West, for registering the culturally anchored ambivalences that resonate within and among identities" (1992:25).

This close association between outward appearances and a sense of self is a recurrent theme in analyses of fashion. According to Quentin Bell (1976:19), "our clothes are too much a part of us for most of us ever to be entirely indifferent to their condition: it is as though the fabric were indeed a natural extension of the body or even of the soul". However, it is not just as a mirror of the self that fashion has been linked with individuality. Davis thinks clothes express our political affiliations, national identity, sexual proclivities and much more:

> Were it the case, as some scholars have maintained, that fashion's sole symbolic end was registering and re-registering invidious distinctions of higher and lower, or better and lesser — that is, distinctions of class and social status — it would hardly have enough "to talk about"; certainly not enough to account for its having thrived in Western society for as long as it has. But [...] it dies have more to say: about our masculinity and femininity, our youth and age, our sexual scruples or lack thereof, our work and play, our politics, national identity and religion. (Davis, 1992:77)

As a visual metaphor, clothing is considered capable of communicating emotions. Veblen always argued that fashion expresses hostility and interclass rivalry, for conspicuous consumption readily lends itself to the demonstration of competition. Francine du Plessix Gray (1981) restates the view that fashion is a tool of envy. She recalls how Coco Chanel's wealthy clients were urged to wear cheap costume jewellery as a way of signalling disdain for *arriviste* posturing. Once the fashion caught on, however, those who owned real jewel retrieved them from bank vaults and wore them as primary symbols of social status, thus indicating the way in which fashion is used to express social contempt.

(Excerpted from Joanne Finkelstein: *Fashion: An Introduction*, NYU Press, 1998)

References

Barthes, R. *The Fashion System*. New York: Jonathan Cape, 1985.

Bell, Q. *Of Human Finery*. London: Hogarth Press, 1976.

Bourdieu, P. *Distinction: A Social Critique of the Judgment of Taste*. Cambridge, Massachusetts: Harvard University Press, 1984.

Davis, F. *Fashion, Culture, and Identity*. Chicago: University of Chicago Press, 1992.

du Plessix Gray, F. "The Escape from Fashion". 1981. 9:43-47.

Hollander, A. *Seeing Through Clothes*. New York: Avon, 1980.

Lévi-Strauss, C. *The Savage Mind*. London: Weidenfeld and Nicolson, 1972.

Lurie, A. *The Language of Clothes*. London: Bloomsbury, 1992.

Sahlins, M. *Culture and Practical Reason*. Chicago: University of Chicago Press, 1976.

Questions

1. According to Finkelstein, "clothes somehow have the power of articulation, that appearances 'speak'", what does it mean?
2. What does it mean by using the metaphor of Regan's using a red tie?
3. Finkelstein says both Barthes and Levi-struss "recognize the fluidities and ambiguities inherent in the structure of fashionable appearance force its codes to remain open-ended". Are the meanings of signs stable/fixed or subjected to change? Can you give any examples?
4. Do you agree with Marshall Sahlins' structuralist perspective of fashion "that colour (light or dark), hue (bright or dull), texture

(rough or smooth), direction (horizontal or vertical) and line (straight or curved) all serve to encode in clothes the fundamental cultural distinctions of gender, status, age, occupation, lifestyle, ethnicity, and sexuality, and they do so in ways which are largely unrecognized and unconscious". Can you give examples to illustrate your point?

5. What is Davis' view of fashion? Do you agree with him? Illustrate your viewpoint with examples.
6. Does the fashion language speak of the individual identity?

Passage 2

Fashion and Identity

Fashion and dress have a complex relationship to identity: on the one hand the clothes we choose to wear can be expressive of identity, telling others something about our genders, class, status and so on; on the other, our clothes cannot always be "read", since they do not straightforwardly "speak" and can therefore be open to misinterpretation. This tension between clothes as revealing and clothes as concealing of identity runs through much of the literature on fashion and fits into broader thematic concerns with identity described by Sennett (1977), Finkelstein (1991) and others. These theorists examine the ways in which identity can be said to be "immanent" in appearance and yet, how it can also be mistaken, hidden behind a "disguise". This tension is felt particularly strongly in the modern city, where, without tradition or established patterns for recognizing others, we mingle with crowds of "strangers" and have only fleeting moments to impress one another. Thus,

when we encounter a stranger as initially mysterious and

> inaccessible, we refer to clothing styles and physical appearance, in the absence of any other means, as a reliable sign of identity. Clothing is frequently seen as symbolic of the individual's status and morality, whether actual or contrived. (Finkelstein, 1991:128)

Anonymity increases the emphasis placed upon appearance and indeed, with the development of large sprawling cities in Europe in the nineteenth century, two strategies for dealing with the anonymity of the city begin to pull in opposite directions: the idea that character is immanent in appearance (Finkelstein, 1991), an idea that pulls one in search of the authenticity of the "other", the "truth" behind the appearance; and an alternative desire for artifice and play with appearance, through fashion and disguise, provoked by the anonymous nature of the city. The contradiction between these two strategies serves to heighten the drama of the city and focuses attention on the body and on dress as indicators to be read for hidden meaning. In the figures of the dandy and the Romantic one finds the contradiction between artifice and authenticity played out through styles of dress. For Campbell (1989), the figures of the dandy and the Romantic in the 19th century represented two divergent practices of dress and consumption which co-existed. The dandy style was an older aristocratic style of dress which articulated a concern for individual distinction, a never ending concern to appear "distinguished", while the Romantic style represents a more familiar desire within contemporary culture, namely to be an expressive individual and be "true to oneself". Thus the dandy style emphasized the artifice of appearance, the self as performed and perfected through self-conscious use of dress and the body, while the Romantic style was concerned with authenticity and the self as "genuine" and "natural".

This tension between artifice and authenticity, between the self as constructed and self-styled and the self as natural and authentic is one that recurs in contemporary literature. As Finkelstein (1991) argues, there is a fundamental contradiction running through our contemporary readings of appearance and identity: while we look to read the other through appearance and hope we can do so accurately, at the very same time we are aware that "appearance can be deceptive". This awareness of the problematic nature of appearance does not stop us from attempting to control how we look and calculate our appearance in order to "put our best face forward" or "make a good impression", and we employ a whole host of strategies to enhance our appearance. Fashion and dress are the tools for this calculation, but various health projects, such as diet, fitness exercises and cosmetic surgery all contribute to the appearance of the body as well. Featherstone (1991a), Giddens (1991) and others have argued that these body projects are an indication of the way in which the self in late modern culture is increasingly a "reflexive self" who is increasingly called upon to think about and act upon the self in particular ways. This theme can also be found in Foucault's work (1988) on "technologies of the self", in which he examines the historically specific ways we are called upon to make ourselves particular sorts of human beings. Different styles of dress can be said to form part of these "technologies of self". In this respect, the dandy and the Romantic can be said to be two 19th-century "technologies of the self" both derived from particular styles of dress as well as owing much to different social and political allegiances.

However, the opinions open for the performance of identity are not unconstrained. How we perform our identity has something to do with our location in the social world as members of particular groups, classes, cultural communities. The clothes we choose to wear represent a compromise between the demands of the social world, the milieu in which we belong, and our own individual desires. "Fashions are bonds that link individuals in a mutual act of conformity to social conventions" (Finkelstein, 1991: 122). This tension between social structure and individual agency is a familiar one to sociologists and is described succinctly by Simmel in his account of "individuality and social forms" (1971). As one of the few sociologists to consider fashion, Simmel accords it some degree of importance in modern society as a phenomenon which exhibits the contradictory desires for social imitation and individual differentiation. Fashion embraces not only the desire to imitate others and to express commonality, but to express individuality. In other words, while dress signals our membership to particular communities and express shared values, ideas and lifestyle, at the same time we do not want to be "clones" dressed in identical fashion to our friends. In order to understand how fashion and dress are linked to identity, Simmel's analysis, with its emphasis on these contradictory tendencies is pertinent here.

Simmel's analysis points to the essentially social nature of dress: individuals are located within communities and their style of dress expresses this belonging. Thus, a further theme when discussing identity in relation to the fashioned body is how fashion and dress articulate group identities, in particular, how they are deployed in order to mark out distinctions between classes and groups of people. This issue touches on questions of status and how status is embodied through fashion, dress and deportment and returns us to discussions of how the body has come to be the bearer of social status. This theme is discussed in Chapters 1 and 3 (in particular through the work of Elias 1978 and Bourdieu 1984, 1994). The importance of the body as the bearing of status and distinction is a theme also explored by Bourdieu (1984, 1994). In his analysis of class, status and power, he argues that the body holds a crucial place as the mediator of this information through inscriptions, tastes and practices he refers to as "habitus". Bourdieu's account looks at how this battle for distinction is a battle for power — economic, social and symbolic — since to acquire distinction potentially raises one's stakes: a Sloane Ranger at a Swiss finishing school who cultivates certain manners and cultural knowledge, stands to increase her socio-economic position by "marrying well".

It is impossible to talk of status and status competition without talking of class. At one time, indeed until as recently as the twentieth century, class was visible through particular uniforms and styles of dress: butchers, bakers, milkmaids, coal miners, were clearly identifiable through dress. However, even in the 19th century new social classes were already pushing forward and competing for status, old and fixed ideas of class were fast disappearing. In contemporary western culture class is no longer so readily apparent to the eye through dress alone but this is not to say that social divisions are no longer apparent through styles of dress: it is still the case that dress can mark out divisions between different groups, and this is particularly true in the case of youth subcultures. Subcultures use dress along with other popular cultural artefacts to mark out differences of taste, lifestyle and identity. However if distinction is about setting oneself apart, it is also always about signalling to others that one is similar to them. Thus the particular manners and bodily dispositions of a Sloane Ranger signal her belonging to a particular class. These themes can be applied to look at how other social groups, such as subcultures, deploy cultural goods to distinguish themselves from each other and from "mainstream" culture. Further, the Sloane Ranger and the member of the youth subculture illustrate the tension described by Simmel (1971), between imitation and differentiation: both set themselves apart from others through bodily style and dress *while also* showing their membership of a particular cultural community by dressing in a similar way to their class or subcultural group.

[...] I then explore in detail the themes outlined above: imitation and differentiation; artifice and authenticity; body, dress and social status.

(Excerpted from Joanne Entwistle's *The Fashioned Body: Fashion, Dress and Modern Social Theory*. Polity Press, 2000.)

References

Bourdieu, P. *Distinction: A Social Critique of the Judgement of Taste*. Cambridge, Massachusetts: Harvard University Press, 1984.

Bourdieu, P. "Structures, Habitus and Practices". In *The Polity Reader in Social Theory*, Edited by P. Press. Cambridge: Polity Press, 1994.

Campbell, C. *The Romantic Ethic and the Spirit of Modern Consumerism*. Oxford: Basil Blackwell, 1989.

Elias, N. *The History of Manners: The Civilizing Process*. Vol. 1. New York: Pantheon, 1978.

Featherstone, M. "The Body in Consumer Society". In *The Body: Social Process and Cultural Theory*, Edited by M. Featherstone, M. Hepworth and B. Turner. London: Sage, 1991a.

Finkelstein, J. *The Fashioned Self*. Cambridge: Polity Press, 1991.

Foucault, M. "Technologies of the Self". In *Technologies of the Self: A Seminar with Michel Foucault*, Edited by L. Martin, H. Gutman and P. Hutton. Amherst: University of Massachusetts Press, 1988.

Giddens, A. *Modernity and Self-Identity: Self and Society in the Late Modern Age*. Cambridge: Polity Press, 1991.

Senett, R. *The Fall of Public Man*. Cambridge: Cambridge University Press, 1977.

Simmel, G. "Fashion". In *On Individuality and Social Forms*, Edited by D. Levine. London: University of Chicago Press, 1971.

Questions

1. Do clothes always show one's "authentic" self and social status? How do we understand fashion as the "technology of self" ?
2. What does the "imitation" behavior in fashion mean?
3. How do we understand the theme of "differentiation" in fashion? Is it possible to dress the body to differentiate one's self?
4. Fashion and dress are linked to social identity in complex ways. Please explain this complexity.

Part II Branding and Culture

Passage 3

Advertising and Brand Equity

To understand the relationships between advertising and brand equity, it pays to first understand just what we mean by a "brand". The original meaning of the word "brand" seems to derive from an Old Norse word *brandr*, which meant "to burn" (Interbrand Group, 1992). Yet in the etymology of the word, this idea of branding as a "permanent mark deliberately made with hot iron" now takes second place to "goods of particular name or trade mark" (Oxford English Dictionary, 1990). But this really does describe a brand as a "name, term, sign, symbol, or design, or a combination of them intended to identify the goods and services of one seller or group of sellers and differentiate them from those of competitors." The AMA definition reminds us of the *reason* for a brand: to enable a person to identify one alternative from a competitor. All of this is true, but a brand must be a *label* in the true sense of that word: something "attached to an object to give information about it"

(Oxford English Dictionary, 1990). But how is that information communicated?

1. The Nature of Brands

When we think of brands, we usually think of products we buy: Coke, Cadbury, Ford, Hoover, Persil, and Mars. But just about anything can be "branded." Products, services, corporations, retail stores, cities, organizations, even individuals can be seen as "brands." Remember, a brand name is meant to embody information something, information that represents an added value, differentiating it in a marked way from alternatives. A brand name is meant to trigger in memory positive associations with that brand. Politicians, hospitals, entertainers, football clubs, corporations, all want their name, their *brand*, to mean something very specific to their market. It is how they wish to be seen, and how they wish to be distinguished from competitive alternatives.

2. Brand Attitude

A brand does provide *information*. But what kind of information does a brand provide, and where does it come from? Think about some brands you know. What comes to mind when you think of them? No doubt a great deal more than the fact that it is a particular product. Perhaps you were thinking about how much you like it, that it is well-known, or that it is "one of the best." All of these thoughts reflect what we call *brand attitude*. A brand name represents everything a person knows about a particular product and what it means to them. It provides a convenient summary of their feelings, knowledge and experience with the brand. It means they do not need to spend a great deal of time "researching" a product each time they are considering a purchase. A person's evaluation of a product is immediately reconstructed from memory, cued by the brand name.

3. Brand Equity

The effect of a positive brand attitude leads to something marketers call *brand equity*. What exactly is brand equity? Most marketers would agree that it is that "something" attached to a brand that adds value over and above the objective characteristics of the product or service. Whatever that "something" is, it is embodied in people's attitudes towards that brand. It is dynamic, and subject to change over time. It attaches itself to the brand name, providing a current summary of people's feelings, knowledge and experience with that product or service.

Think of chocolate for a minute. Basically, chocolate is chocolate. Or is it? Are some *brands* better than others? Why? What about washing-up powder? They all get the job done, and use the basic ingredients. Or do you think some do a better job than others? What about toothpaste, or vodka, or underwear? Where do the differences among brands in these product categories come from? How much of the difference is "real" versus perceived? Why do you prefer one brand over another, especially if when looked at with a coldly objective eye, there is very little, if any, actual difference in the products?

4. Brand Positioning

At its most general, a brand position is a "supercommunication" effect that tells the consumer what the brand is, who it is for, and what it offers. This reflects the relationship between brand positioning and the two core communication effects of brand awareness and brand attitude. It's easy to understand that one must have strong awareness if a brand is to be considered when the "need" for that type of product (however the *consumer* defines it) occurs. Strong brand awareness (for almost any brand) must be generated and sustained with marketing communication. It is marketing communication, and advertising in particular, that builds and maintains *brand salience*. It is not enough for a brand to be recognized if it is to be successful. A brand must occupy a "salient" position within the consumer's consideration set. In fact, the strength of a brand's salience is one indicator of the brand's equity. (A useful measure of this is the ratio of top-of-mind recall to total recall among competitive brands in a category.)

Brand attitude, however, is not quite so easy to deal with. Who exactly is the target audience? Is everyone looking for the same thing; of the same things all the time? What is important, and to whom? How are brands seen to deliver on the things important to the target audience? Answers to these questions are critical if we are to positively effect brand attitude.

The role of benefits in effective positioning in communication is of course essential. But benefits must be considered in relationship to brand attitude, which in its turn is the link to purchase motive. Consumers hold that what we might think of as an overall summary judgement about a brand, following the Expectancy-Value notion of attitude: "Hush Puppies makes great shoes" is an *attitude* about Hush Puppies that connects the brand in the consumer's mind with what is the likely purchase motive, sensory gratification (i. e. they buy Hush Puppies to *enjoy* them). This brand attitude, however, which we might think of as a "superbelief," doesn't just spring from nowhere, but is the result of one or more beliefs about the *specific benefits* the brand is thought by the consumer to offer in support of that overall attitude. Effective communication strategy requires an understanding of what that belief structure is, and how it builds brand attitude.

Within the overall positioning that results from this understanding, one we must determine what the benefit emphasis and focus should be

(Percy, Rossiter, and Elliott, 2001). To begin with, it is important to remember that purchase motive is really the *underlying* basis of benefit. Purchase motives are, after all, the fundamental "energizers" of buyer behavior. These same motives also energize the usage of products. Motive-based positioning requires a *correct* answer to the question of why consumers in the category are *really* buying particular *brands*. Unfortunately, most benefits tend to be motivationally ambiguous.

One must also be careful to distinguish between motives that drive product category decisions rather than brand decisions. People may buy (say) active casual footwear because they are comfortable (a negative motive), but buy particular brands for more "style" related reasons (a positive motive). This is an absolutely critical distinction. Benefits like comfort or low price relate to negative motives, and are unlikely to drive *specific brand* purchases. Yet, someone may be looking for a good price in the category, but *not* at the expense of "style." The reason this is such an important point is that positive motives suggest marketing communication where the execution itself actually becomes the product benefit. Here more than ever a truly unique execution is required where the brand owns the "feeling" created by the advertisers for the brand. You can't "prove" you have a more "stylish" or popular shoe, but you can make people *believe* you do.

(Excerpted from Larry Percy's paper "Advertising and Brand Equity", in *Branding and Advertising*, Ed. by Flemming Hansen & Lars Bech Christensen, Copenhagen Business School Press, 2003.)

References

Interbrand G. *World's Greatest Brands: An International Review*. New York: John Wiley, 1992.

Oxford E. D. Oxford: Oxford University Press, 1990.

Percy, L., Rossiter, J. R., & Elliott, R. *Strategic Advertising Management*.

Usa: Oxford University Press, 2001.

Questions

1. What is a brand?
2. What is the nature of a brand?
3. What is brand equity? How important is it to the value of goods?
4. How would you define brand attitude, brand positioning/identity and brand personality?

Passage 4

Branding with Culture

Brands are molded with cultural elements. It is the spirit of culture endowed in brands that is communicating with the targeted consumers. Without cultural conceptions brands are soulless and powerless. The following part concerning branding the bottled water is a good example to show how cultural meanings are fused into brands to promote consumption.

Years ago, advertising executive could jokingly praise an expert by saying that he or she "could sell ice-cubes to Eskimos". Now that kind of feat, getting people to pay for things that they already have in abundance around them, for which they have no manifest need, has become commonplace. Today marketers recognize that goods have magical powers that have nothing to do with "needs", and they have become magicians who transform mundane and abundant things into exotic valuables.

Bottled water is an exceptionally clear example of the power of branding to make commodities a meaningful part of daily life. Of course, brands are not themselves empty bottles, filled with magic by the all powerful tools of advertising and marketing. As many recent theorists and critics have shown, brands have a history and cultural life that makes them more than puppets; each brand is a collaborative construction by many parties. Water, because it is so ubiquitous and mundane, exposes the complexity of this collaboration particularly well. [...]

1. History, Nature and Cultural Meaning

Both those selling water in bottles and those for whom water is a universal right portray water as a substance that comes from nature. Water is more than a symbol of the natural world; it is usually seen as the very substance of the natural world. Nature, after all, has been likened to a popular secular religion in the West (Dunlap, 2004). In western Europe there are deep historical roots for the idea that water has magical power to heal and confer vitality, power rooted in sacred springs and wells that were seen as sources of spiritual knowledge and wisdom (Strang, 2004: 98). The power of water to connect people to the power of nature was transmitted through the contagious magic of baptism, libation, bathing and drinking, both in pagan and Christian traditions.

On top of this long tradition, we can identify another historical layer of meaning that emerges from the scientific project of defining and measuring water, and the modernist industrial theme of "control of water" as the mastery or conquest of nature (Hamlin, 2000). Heroic films about the damming of great rivers and the damming of floods expressed the power of industrial society over untamed nature. Modernism imposes human will (and governmentality) on nature by channeling, damming, chemical treatment, purification and organized distribution. Because today bottled water can draw on both traditions, it has the unusual capacity to carry and transmit the magic and power of nature and modern technology at the same time. In a world where floods and tidal waves still prove the imperfection of human control over the natural power of water, every bottle of water is a visual metaphor for control and at the same time a reminder that, without water, people cannot exist.

Part of the cultural power of water is rooted in the geographic and class associations of early brands of mineral water, which carried the prestige and magical healing power of famous spas to the dinning tables of the rich and sophisticated. These spas in turn were founded at the sites of ancient springs and wells which people had visited for centuries to be blessed, healed and fortified. Perrier and Vichy, both associated with spas, are now brands so venerable that they have themselves been embedded in cultural meanings, associated with healing and the tables of the elite. They have even become generic synonyms for any kind of mineral water, like Kleenex for tissue and Coke for Cola drinks. Once they achieved this generic status their mystique could be mobilized, so they retain their authenticity even detached from place. These old brands led the way in transferring the magic of springs and pools from original "natural" sites to spas, national companies and the global corporations. They still draw on the power of nature, but their value is now bolstered by the certificates and scientific testimonials on their labels.

In the early age of branding, individual trusted agents were able to use their own names as the magic that could guarantee quality and efficacy. Thus in 1826 the Quaker John Horniman personally warranted the quality of the first packaged teas ever sold in England by putting his name on each package after it was sealed (Rappaport, 2006). While 18th-century products were known mostly by their place of origin (Burgundy wine, Yorkshire ham, China tea), in the 19th-century the same product required a personalized agent to carry them from producer to market (e. g. Libby's meat, Huntley & Palmer biscuits). It is noteworthy that water was never personalized this way, retaining its connection to the source, suggesting that water's powers still came from nature, rather than from its agent. This may be why most waters continue to be sold by reference to places and natural origins (e. g. glaciers, springs, islands, states), instead of by personal brand names. There are no successful personally branded celebrity waters, or highly technological "artificial" waters. ①

Most water advertising and labeling today uses images from nature, especially the mountains that formed the first major object of romantic European nature-worship in the late 18th- and early 19th-centuries. The predominant color for labels is blue, and bottles are almost always transparent — you never see water in brown bottles. But this form of nature is still, like medicinal waters with their long lists of minerals, mediated by scientific artifice. A typical example is an advertisement for RealPure, which says its water is "straight from the source at Real Pure's state-of-the-art plant atop a natural spring." ② A 1999 report by the National Resources Defense Council (NRDC) gleaned a list of key words used by water brands on labels, or in marketing, of which some of the most common were "pure", "pristine", and "natural".

Some have argued that nature has recently become a kind of "super commodity", that provides a kind of connection between consumers and producers that has largely been lost in the confusion of industrial capitalism (Descola and Palsson, 1996). But there are clearly many aspects of nature (and water) that resist commodification, and it is just this resistance that makes Perrier water bottled at the ancient source, or

---

① It might appear that reverse osmosis or desalinated water are exceptions, but in the marketplace both are low-value tap-water substitutes rather than branded high-value products. A good example of natural sourcing to a famous locale is Loch Ness water, announced at http://www. beverageworld. com/. beverageworld/ headlines/article_display. jsp? vnu_content_id = 1000673392.

② This advertisement appears in *Beverage Industry News*, April 2002.

Lourdes water in a tiny vial, or fresh spring water from a mountain fresher different from the generic stuff flowing from the tap. At the same time, while most consumers in rich countries may enjoy the *thought* of pure water flowing in a mountain stream, most would be terrified to actually *drink* it without some kind of purification.

2. New Cultural Horizons

Given all the rich meanings and associations, and the manifest social and ideological dangers presented by water, how do companies actually sell water in the marketplace? They have built on the positive historical meanings of water, but they have also appealed to other aspects of body and identity which rival the importance of the cultural realms of risk, health, and nature. Most obvious of these are social distinctions of wealth and class, which have after all been used for centuries to sell European bottled water in restaurants around the world. Now there are much finer gradations of price and perceived quality, from unbranded generic bulk water in large refillable containers and mass-market treated tap-waters sold by large soft-drink companies, through the "mid-market" and onward to more expensive and exotic "premium" brands. The basic social distinctions of age and gender are also reflected in the marketing of water for male athletes, water "specifically formulated for a woman's special needs", and brands for children (vitamin-fortified Kid Fuel in small blue bottles for boys and pink for girls) and active teens.

Health as a cultural realm in the West is also an arena for the conflict between nature and science, and while some waters advertise their natural sources, others make health claims based on scientific additives. In the USA there are now several brands like Physique Power Water, "enhanced with 'nutraceuticals'"; there are also vitamin waters, nicotine, aspirin and caffeine waters, sports water, "smart" water, a "diet" water called Skinny, and even a special water for pets.

Some of these products make extravagant claims, like "eVamor alkaline artesian water", which "works to neutralize acid and delivers antioxidants and minerals that burn fat" (ad in *Beverage Industry News*, May 2003). ①

Cross-cultural studies by anthropologists have found that in a wide variety of cultures, rare substances with distant, exotic origins are especially powerful, and are often the source of medicines with extraordinary powers to affect the body (Helms, 1988; Taussig, 1987). While globalization has broken down the effects of distance to some extent, its power still adheres to water from distant places, such as icebergs and glaciers, and there are still rare additives including ancient air bubbles from deep inside glaciers and flakes of gold.

Modern consumer culture is full of devices that maintain the exclusive, exotic and mysterious nature of goods to enhance their value. To understand some of the richness and variety of value-enhancing exoticizing modes, I asked a roomful of about 25 marketing professionals, professors and graduate students in a major US business school to think of new ways to sell water. Within 15 minutes they produced a long list that included the following:

- water from each of the great rivers of the world;
- meltwater from named glaciers, or assorted waters from sets of glaciers in a region, which become more expensive as the glaciers get smaller;
- cave water, including water from the deepest, longest, darkest, etc.;
- great underground aquifers — in the USA many have heard of the

---

① Another recent "diet water" is the Skinny Water widely marketed in the USA as a 100% natural European artesian water (http://www.skinnywater.com/).

great Oglala aquifer;

- carbon-dated and fossil waters, for example water that last fell to earth 6 million years ago;
- oasis water — from the famous deserts such as the Sahara, Gobi and Kalahari;
- water gathered from particular named storms and hurricanes, with the potential for collection sets, or keeping special vintages;
- water from the childhood homes of movie stars, the water that made them who they are today;
- kinky waters — from the island of Lesbos for example;
- waters of the seven continents;
- waters for different parts of the body — stomach, skin, hair water.

Some of the group's suggestions were already on the market, for example water for particular sports such as football and tennis, event-waters labeled for a wedding, a funeral, or a special gathering, patriotic water (popular in the USA after 9 · 11), and personalized water with your name or the name of your organization or company on the label. Since the time I performed this experiment, I am sure some of the others have appeared, because new water brands and products are entering the US market at the rate of about eight per month, compared with five per month for soft drink. ①

The most intriguing thing about this list is that almost all of them depend on very old forms of value which would have been familiar to 16th-century Europeans, the ancient Greeks and Romans, and many of the ancient and contemporary cultures discussed by Taussig and Helms

① These figures are taken from *Beverage Industry News* (2002). By comparison the rate of introduction of new brands was much higher in alcoholic drinks — 34 new products a month.

(1993, 1998) in his work on the powers of exotic goods. Each one in some way manipulates *distance*, either increasing or decreasing it in geography, time, or social proximity. Geographically, value adheres to places to places far away (deserts), or those that present the consumer's own imagined location (USA, hometown). Fossil water from the distant past stretches time, in contrast to the immediate present represented by water from a particular wedding. Personal water is the "zero point" of social distance, while water associated with celebrities or royalty maximizes the social gap. Taussig has argued that the values of exoticism that are being used here are based on the universal propensity for humans to build value around relations of mimesis and alterity, identity and difference (Taussig, 1993). This in turn can be linked to Simmel's much earlier distinction between identity and individuality (Wolff, 1950).

Another principal at work here is McCracken's well-known "Diderot Effect", where objects are formed into sets, with the implication that a complete set (seven continents) has much more values than the total of all its parts. Buying one of the set can then easily lead into an exploration of the entire group, and this can even build upwards into "sets of sets" or higher ranked sets, in the progression well-known to those who study collecting. Again this is an ancient principal in human relationships with material culture that probably pre-dates the market; ancient Mayan nobles seem to have collected "sets" of potty from particular artists and workshops.

None of these principles that give value to water is specific to water as a commodity, or even to market societies, the West, or modern times. But all of these meanings have today been captured by commodities, and as such they are all antithetical to any ideal of water as a free good, a natural right and therefore the absolute opposite of a commodity. This is the contradiction that leads to resistance to any kind of bottling, branding, labeling, advertising and selling of water in commodity packages. This points out that in some ways it's the wrapper, the label and the packaging that elicit resistance, not the water itself. This may be why there is so little protest over the long-standing practice (in the USA at least) of selling large refillable plastic containers of purified water to business and homes for "coolers". Here the water is a commodity, but it has its own specialized container, very much *unlike* the bottles and cans that other "drinks" are sold in. Water only becomes transgressive and elicits resistance when it is sold like any other beverage. The point of the resistance is exactly that water *is not* like any other beverage.

(Excerpted from Richard Wilk: "Bottled Water: The Pure Commodity in the Age of Branding", *Journal of Consumer Culture*, 2006, 6: 303.)

Notes

These names are registered trademarks: Perrier, Vichy, Kleenex, Coke, Colgate, RealPure, Evian, Nike, Kid Fuel, Skinny, eVamor, Coca-Cola, McDonald's, Dasani.

References

Descola, P. and Palsson, G. (Eds) *Nature and Society: Anthropological Perspectives*. London: Routledge, 1996.

Dunlap, T. R. *Faith in Nature: Environmentalism as Religious Quest*. Seattle, WA: University of Washington Press, 2004.

Hamlin, C. 'Waters' or 'Water'? Master in Water History and Their Implications for Contemporary Water Policy. *Water Policy*, 2000, 2: 313-325.

Helms, M. *Ulysses' Sail: An Ethnographic Odyssey of Power, Knowledge, and Geographical Distance*. Princeton, NJ: Princeton

University Press, 1988.

Rappaport, E. D. "Packaging China: Foreign Articles and Dangerous Tastes in the Mid-Victorian Tea Party". In *The Making of the Consumer: Knowledge, Power and Identity in the Modern World*, Edited by Frank Trentmann. Oxford: Berg, 2006.

Strang, V. *The Meaning of Water*. Oxford: Berg, 2004.

Taussig, M. *Shamanism, Colonialism and the Wild Man: A Study in Terror and Healing*. Chicago: Chicago University Press, 1987.

Taussig, M. *Mimesis and Alterity: A Particular History of the Senses*. London: Routledge, 1993.

Wolff, K. (Ed., Translator). *The Sociology of George Simmel*. Glencoe, IL: Free Press, 1950.

Questions

1. What does it mean by "selling ice-cubes to Eskimos"? Are ice-cubes easily available to Eskimos? Do Eskimos need to buy ice-cubes as commodities?
2. What is the difference between bottled water sold in the market and the water available to people in the world?
3. What is used to brand the bottled water or what is connected to the power of water?
4. What specific meanings in relation to nature are used to label the water?
5. What kinds of water brands are successful, water with reference to places and natural origins, or water branded by celebrities and water represented as of technological production?
6. Why are "new cultural horizons" explored by marketing and advertising personnel? In the bottled water market, is water sold or the cultural power of water?
7. What cultural elements are popular nowadays in consumer culture, as

can be seen in the list of new ways to sell water?

Part III Fashioning and Branding Youth Culture

Passage 5

Youth Subculture, Style and Self

Youth subculture consists of a relatively stable symbolic system and life experiences shared, maintained and transformed by youth but made to be distinctive from their parents' culture on which they are dependent, on the other hand, this symbolic system and the life experiences are opposed to the dominant culture in a given time and society.

When we talk about youth subculture nowadays, we often refer to the widely recognized but ridiculed mass youth culture since the late 1950s, going through the 1960s and lasting until the 1970s. During this period, youth adopted unique, special and spectacular clothing and hair style in both Britain (the Teds) and the U. S. (the Beats), made use of the car as the private space of life for courtship, sex, drinking and listening to the radio, especially to the suburban and rural youth in the U. S. who desired for the freedom of roaming on the road and the experience of the cities. In the 1960s, subcultures proliferated with the participation of college students who largely became "hippies". More subcultural groups appeared in Britain including the Mods, Rockers, Skinheads. These groups participated in mass protests against military service, social restrictions on speech as well as other forms of radical political activities, indulging themselves in drug addiction and sexual experiments.

Critics of cultural studies think highly of youth subculture by studying style and the ways of life created by youth in relation to factors of class, ethnicity, gender, sexuality, etc.

Dick Hebdige through a semiotic investigation of the signs of style, or objects produced by youth (i. e. dress, music, hair) in relation to gender, ethnicity and age, in *Subculture: the Meaning of Style* (1979), argues that subculture represents subversion of normalcy and deviant reactions of subordinate groups to challenge hegemony of the dominant culture and the society controlled by adults. In his analysis, Hebdige highlights the style as the signifying practice to "reflect, express and resonate [...] aspects of group life" (Quoted in Hebdige, 1979: 114), and attempts to disclose its message or the intended meaning as well as the position of the speaking subject by exploring the styled objects of various subculture groups together with their art of construction. Style is a tactic to articulate against socio-cultural oppression upon the youth. As Hebdige claims, "style in subculture is, then pregnant with significance" (Hebdige, 1979: 18) as the objects "can be magically appropriated, 'stolen' by subordinate groups and made to carry 'secret' meanings which express, in code, a form of resistance to the order which guarantees their continued subordination." (1979: 18)

One important style of subculture is bricolage (Hebdige, 1979: 102)— "reordering and re-contextualization of objects to communicate fresh meanings, within a total system of significances, which already includes prior and sedimented meanings attached to the objects used" (Clarke et al., 1975: 177). In other words, bricolage means taking the objects away from their original contexts and juxtaposing them together in a new context without any logical necessity to effect new symbolic meanings. As subcultural style is characterized by such a technique, existing materials/objects are used by youth to communicate meanings and to create a new, different identity for themselves.

Stuart Hall and Tony Jefferson also approach the meaning of subculture through the analysis of the meaning of style. They consider youth subculture as symbolic attempts to resist the dominant bourgeois power in the capitalist society by deliberate adoption of the behavior and style that seem to be threatening to the society under capitalist control. They articulate based on the notions of hegemony and class structure that the working-class youth like the skinheads resolved to make use the objects and images of negative meanings (e. g. shaved head image) in the dominant cultural code and brought them into new meanings to create for themselves an identity different from existing social groups, because of their resistant attitude to the dominant class and hegemonic culture,

> This registering of group identity, situation and trajectory in a visible style both consolidates the group from a loosely-focused to a tightly—bounded entity: and sets the group off, distinctively, from other similar and dissimilar groups. Indeed, like all other kinds of cultural construction, the symbolic use of things to consolidate and express an internal coherence was, in the same moment, a kind of implied opposition to (where it was not an active and conscious contradiction of) other groups against which its identity was defined. This process led, in our period, to the distinctive visibility of those groups which pressed the "subcultural solution" to its limits along this stylistic path. (Clarke *et. al.*, 1976:56-57)

So the subculture style created by youth assumes their position of "opposition" or the symbolic resistance to the hegemonic/dominant culture of the capitalist society. Thus youth, as considered by critics, represents "a metaphor for social change" (Clarke *et. al.*, 1976: 17).

Commercialization of Youth Subculture

Capitalists perceive the business potential of youth culture and the great market of youth, youth subculture is appropriated for consumption. Then, while some subculture style (e.g. the subversive allure of punk subculture is promoted as the Cool by the fashion industry) is incorporated into the mainstream culture and accepted as the mainstream taste by the masses now, other subcultures reject or modify the importance of style, stressing membership through the adoption of an ideology which may be much more resistant to commercial exploitation. In fact, the process of appropriation and commercialization of youth subculture may often result in the death or evolution of the subculture, as its members may adopt new styles that appear alien to mainstream society. This process provides a constant stream of styles which may be commercially adopted.

References

Clarke, J., Hall, S., Jefferson, T. & Roberts, B. "Subcultures, Cultures and Class", In *Resistance Through Rituals: Youth Subcultures in Postwar Britain*. London: Hutchinson, 1976.

Hebdige, D. *Subculture: the Meaning of Style*. Routledge, 1979.

Questions

1. What is youth subculture?
2. How do cultural critics think of youth subculture since the 1950s?
3. Do you think youth subculture today still keeps the meaning of social revolt today? Why?

Passage 6

Branding with Youth Culture

1. Marketing at Youth

Roberts isn't the only one who holds this view. *Advertising Age* reporter Jeff Jensen goes so far as to make the claim that for today's young people, "Selling out is not only accepted, it's considered hip. "① To object would be, well, unhip. There is no need to further romanticize the original Woodstock. Among (many) other things, it was also a big-label-backed rock festival, designed to turn a profit. Still, the myth of Woodstock as a sovereign youth-culture state was part of a vast project of generational self-definition — a concept that would have been wholly foreign to those in attendance at Woodstock '94, for whom generational identity had largely been a pre-packaged good and for whom the search for self had always been shaped by marketing hype, whether or not they believed it or defined themselves against it. This is a side effect of brand expansion that is far more difficult to track and quantity than the branding of culture and city spaces. This loss of space happens inside the individual; it is a colonization not of physical space but of mental space.

In a climate of youth-marketing feeding frenzy, all culture begins to be created with the frenzy in mind. Much of youth culture becomes suspended in what sociologists Robert Goldman and Stephen Papson call "arrested development," nothing that "we have, after all, no idea of what punk or grunge or hip hop as social and cultural movements might

① "His Replace Jingles on TV Commercials", *Globe and Mail*, 29 November 1997.

look like if they were not mined for their gold [. . .]"① This "mining" has not gone unnoticed or unopposed. Both the anticorporate cultural journal *The Baffler* and the now-defunct *Might* magazine brilliantly lampooned the desperation and striving of the youth-culture industry in the mid-nineties. Dozens, if not hundreds, of zines and websites have been launched and have played no small part in setting the mood for the kind of brand-based attacks. [. . .] For the most part, however, branding's insatiable cultural thirst just creates more marketing. Marketing that thinks it is culture.

2. The Youth Market Saves the Day

[Before the 1990s there was brand crisis/recession]. All that changed in the early nineties when the baby boomers dropped their end of the consumer chain and the brands underwent their identity crisis. At about the time of Marlboro Friday, Wall Street took a closer look at the brands that had flourished through the recession, and noticed something interesting. Among the industries that were holding steady or taking off were bear, soft drinks, fast food and *sneakers* — not to mention chewing gum and Barbie dolls. There was something else: 1992 was the first year since 1975 that the number of teenagers in America increased. Gradually, an idea began to dawn on many in the manufacturing sector and entertainment industries: maybe their sales were slumping not because consumers were "brand-blind", but because these companies had their eyes fixed on the wrong demographic prize. This was not a time for selling Tide and Snuggle to housewives — it was a time for beaming MTV, Nike, Hilfiger, Microsoft, Netscape and *Wired* to global teens and their overgrown imitators. Their parents might have gone bargain

① Robert Goldman and Stephen Papson. *Sign Wars: The Cluttered Landscape of Advertising*. New York: Guilford Press, 1996, p. 43.

basement, but kids, it turned out, were still willing to pay up to fit in. through this process, peer pressure emerged as a powerful market force, making the keeping-up-with-the-Joneses consumerism of their suburban parents pale by comparison. As clothing retailer Elise Decoteau said of her teen shoppers, "They run in packs. If you sell to one, you sell to everyone in their class and everyone in their school."①

There was just one catch. As the success of the branding superstars like Nike had shown, it was not going to be sufficient for companies simply to market their same products to a younger demographic; they need to fashion brand identities that would resonate with this new culture. If they were going to turn their lackluster products into transcendent meaning machines — as the dictates of branding demanded — they would need to remake themselves in the image of nineties cool: its music, styles and politics.

3. Branding and Creating Cool Envy at School

Fueled by dual promises of branding and the youth market, the corporate sector experienced a burst of creative energy. Cool, alternative, young, hip — whatever you want to call it — was the perfect identity for product-driven companies looking to become transcendent image-based brands. Advertisers, brand managers, music, film and television producers raced back to high school, sucking up to the in-crowd in a frantic effort to isolate and reproduce in TV commercials the precise "attitude" teens and twenty-somethings were driven to consume with their snack foods and pop tunes. And as in high schools everywhere, "Am I cool?" became the deeply dull and all-consuming question of every moment, echoing not only through class and

---

① See *Greater Baton Rouge Business Report*, 28 June 1994, 30. Decoteau is co-owner of the store serape in Baton Rouge.

locker rooms, but through the high-powered meetings and conference calls of Corporate High.

The quest for cool is by nature riddled with self-doubt ("Is this cool?" One can hear the legions of teen shoppers nervously quizzing each other. "Do you think this is lame?") Except now the harrowing doubts of adolescence are the billion-dollar questions of our age. The insecurities go round and round the boardroom table, turning ad writers, art directors and CEOs into turbo-powered teenagers, circling in front of their bedroom mirrors trying to look blase. Do the kids think we're cool? Do we have attitude? The *right* attitude?

Cool, it seems, is the make-or-break quality in the 1990s branding. It is the ironic sneer-track of ABC sitcoms and late-night talk shows; it is what sells psychedelic Internet servers, extreme sports gear, ironic watches, mind-blowing fruit juice, kitsch-laden jeans, post-modern sneakers and post-gender colognes. Our "aspirational age," as they say in marketing studies, is about seventeen. This applies equally to the forty-seven-year-old baby.

4. Tommy Hilfiger: To the Ghetto and Back Again

Tommy Hilfiger, even more than Nike or Adidas, has turned the harnessing of ghetto cool into a mass-marketing science. Hilfiger forged a formula that has since been imitated by Polo, Nautica, Munsingwear (thanks to Puff Daddy's fondness for the penguin logo) and several other clothing companies looking for a short cut to making it at the suburban mall with inner-city attitude.

Like a depoliticized, hyper-patriotic Benetton, Hilfiger ads are a tangle of Cape Cod multiculturalism: scrubbed black faces lounging with their wind-swept white brothers and sisters in that great country club in the sky, and always against the backdrop of a billowing American flag. "By respecting one another we can reach all cultures and communities," the company says. "We promote [...] the concept of living the American dream."① But the hard facts of Tommy's interracial financial success have less to do with finding common ground between cultures than with the power and mythology embedded in America's deep racial segregation.

Tommy Hilfiger started off squarely as white-preppy wear in the tradition of Ralph Lauren and Lacoste. But the designer soon realized that his clothes also had a peculiar cachet in the inner cities, where the hip-hop philosophy of "living large" saw poor and working-class kids acquiring status in the ghetto by adopting the gear and accoutrements of prohibitively costly leisure activities, such as skiing, golfing, even boating. Perhaps to better position his brand within this urban fantasy, Hilfiger began to associate his clothes more consciously with these sports, shooting ads at yacht clubs, beaches and other nautical locales. At the same time, the clothes themselves were redesigned to appeal more directly to the hip-hop aesthetic. Cultural theorist Paul Smith describes the shift as "bolder colors, bigger and baggier styles, more hoods and cords, and more prominence for logos and the Hilfiger name."② He also plied rap artists like Snoop Dogg with free clothes and, walking the tightrope between the yacht and the ghetto, launched a line of Tommy Hilfiger beepers.

Once Tommy was firmly established as a ghetto thing, the real selling could begin — not just to the comparatively small market of poor inner-city youth but to the much larger market of middle-class white and Asian kids who mimic black style in everything from lingo to sports to music. Company sales reached $847 million in 1998 — up from a

---

① *Tommy Hilfiger* 1997 *Annual Report*.

② Paul Smith, "Tommy Hilfiger in the Age of Mass Customization", in *No Sweat: Fashion, Free Trade, and the Rights of Garment Workers*, Edited by Andrew Ross. New York: Verso, 1997, p. 253.

paltry $53 million in 1991 while Hilfiger was still, as Smith puts it, "Youth Republican Clothing." Like so much of cool hunting, Hilfiger's marketing journey feeds off the alienation at the heart of America's race relations: selling white youth on their fetishization of black style, and black youth on their fetishization of white wealth.

5. Indie Inc.

Offering *Fortune* magazine readers advice on how to market to teenage girls, reporter Nina Munk writes that "you have to pretend that they're running things. [...] Pretend you still have to be discovered. Pretend the girls are in charge."① Being a huge corporation might sell on Wall Street, but as the brands soon learned on their cool hunt, "indie" was the pitch on Cool Street. Many corporations were unfazed by this shift, coming out with faux indie brands like Politix cigarettes from Moonlight Tobacco (courtesy of Philip again), Old Navy's mock army surplus (the Gap) and OK Cola (Coke).

In an attempt to cash in on the indie marketing craze, even Coke itself, the most recognizable brand name on earth, has tried to go underground. Fearing that it was too establishment for brand-conscious teens, the company launched an ad campaign in Wisconsin that declared Coke the "Unofficial State Drink." The campaign included radio spots that were allegedly broadcast from a pirate radio station called EKOC: Coke backward. Not to be outdone, Gap-owned Old Navy actually did launch its own pirate radio station to promote its brand — a micro-brand transmitter that could only be picked up in the immediate vicinity of one of its Chicago billboards.② And in 1999, when Lévi's decided it was

---

① Nina Munk. "Girl Power", *Fortune*, 8 December 1997, 137.

② "Old Navy Anchors Micro-Radio Billboard", *Chicago Sun-Times*, 28 July 1998.

high time to recoup its lost cool, it also went indie, launching Red Line jeans (no mention of Lévi's anywhere) and K-1 Khakis (no mention of Lévi's or Dockers).

(Ironic Consumption: No Deconstruction Required)

With the tentacles of branding reaching into every crevice of youth culture, leaching brand-image content not only out of street styles like hip-hop but psychological attitudes like ironic detachment, the cool hunt has had to go further afield to find unpilfered space and that left only one frontier: the past.

6. Sell or Be Sold

After almost a decade of the branding frenzy, cool hunting has become an internal contradiction: the hunters must rarefy youth "microcultures" by claiming that only full-time hunters have the know-how to unearth them — or else why hire cool hunters at all? Sputnik warns its clients that if the cool trend is "visible in your neighborhood or crowding your nearest mall, the learning is over. It's too late. [...] You need to get down with the streets, to be in the trenches every day."① And yet this is demonstrably false; so-called street fashions — many of them planted by brandmasters like Nike and Hilfiger from day one — reach the ballooning industry of glossy youth-culture magazines and video stations without a heartbeat's delay. And if there is one thing virtually every young person now knows, it's that street style and youth culture are infinitely marketable commodities.

Besides, even there was a lost indigenous tribe of cool a few years back, rest assured that it no longer exists. It turns out that the prevailing legalized forms of youth stalking are only the tip of the iceberg: the Sputnik vision for the future of hip marketing is for companies to hire

① Lopiano-Misdom and De Luca. *Street Trends*, 8-9.

armies of Sputnik spawns — young "street promoters," "net promoters" and "street distributors" who will hype brands one-on-one on the street, in the clubs and on-line. "Use the magic of peer-to-peer distribution — it worked in the freestyle sport cultures, mainly because the promoters were their friends. [...] Street promoting will survive as the only true means of personally 'spreading the word.'"① So all arrows point to more jobs for the ballooning industry of "street snitches", certified representatives of their demographic who will happily become walking infomercials for Nike, Reebok and Lévi's.

7. Rock-and-Roll CEOs

There is an amusing irony in the fact that so many of our captains of industry pay cool hunters good money to lead them on the path to brand-image nirvana. The true barometers of hip are not the hunters, postmodern admen, the change agents or even those trendy teenagers they're all madly chasing. They are the CEOs themselves, for the most part, so damn rich that they can afford to stay on top of all the coolest culture trends. Guys like Diesel Jeans founder Renzo Rosso, who, according to *Business Week*, "rides to work on a Ducati Monster motorcycle."② Or Nike's Phil Knight, who only took off his ever-present wraparound Oakley sunglasses after Oakley CEO Jim Jannard refused to sell him the company. Or famed admen Dan Wieden and David Kennedy who built a basketball court — complete with bleachers — in their corporate headquarters. Or Virgin's Richard Branson, who launched a London bridal store in a wedding dress, rappelled off the roof of his new Vancouver megastore while uncorking a bottle of champagne and then later crash-landed in the Algerian desert in his hot-air balloon — all

① Lopiano-Misdom and De Luca. *Street Trends*, 110.

② *Business Week*, 12 April 1996.

during the month of December 1996. These CEOs are the new rock stars — and why shouldn't they be? Forever trailing the scent of cool, they are full-time, professional teenagers, but unlike real teenagers, they have nothing to distract them from the hot pursuit of the edge: no homework, puberty, college-entrance exams or curfews for them.

8. Getting Over It

As we will see later on, the sheer voracity of the corporate cool hunt did much to provoke the rise of brand-based activism: through adbusting, computer hacking and spontaneous illegal street parties, young people all over the world are aggressively reclaiming space from the corporate world, "unbranding" it, guerrilla-style. But the effectiveness of the cool hunt also set the stage for anticorporate activism in another way: inadvertently, it exposed the impotence of almost all other forms of political resistance *except* anticorporate resistance, cutting-edge marketing trend at a time.

When the youth-culture feeding frenzy began in the early nineties, many of us who were young at the time saw ourselves as victims of a predatory marketing machine that co-opted our identities, our styles and our ideas and turned them into brand food. Nothing was immune: not punk, not hip-hop, not fetish, not techno — not even, as I'll get to in Chapter 5, campus feminism or multiculturalism. Few of us asked, at least not right away, why it was that these scenes and ideas were proving so packageable, so unthreatening — and so profitable. Many of us had been certain we were doing something subversive and rebellious. [...]

We know advertising is an extreme sport and CEOs are the new rock stars, it's worth remembering that extreme sports are not political movements and rock, despite its historic claims to the contrary, is not revolution. In fact, to determine whether a movement genuinely challenges the structures of economic and political power, one need only measure how affected it is by the goings-on in the fashion and advertising industries. If, even after being singled out as the latest fad, it continues as if nothing had happened, it's a good bet it is a real movement. If it spawns an industry of speculation about whether movement X has lost its "edge," perhaps its adherents should be looking for a sharper utensil. And as we will soon see, that is exactly what many young activists are in the process of doing.

(Excerpted from Normi Klein: *No Logo*, New York: Picador USA, 2001.)

Questions

1. What is Woodstock and what kind of attempt of youth does it represent? What is marketed at youth?
2. How did brands regain their life in the 1990s after their crisis in the 1980s?
3. What is the taste created in school and how is it created? What is the power of "envy"? What is its purpose of creating such taste and envy?
4. How did Tom Hilfiger brand itself? What images or cultural symbols are used in creating its brand?
5. In the part "Sell or Sold", why is cool-hunting so important?
6. What does "Rock-and-Roll CEOs" mean, according to the depictions?
7. Is the "cool hunt" effective? Are youth contented with the trend of cool-branding?
8. In terms of the commercialization of youth culture, what does the author mean to youth culture/movement by the sentence "If it spawns an industry of speculation about whether movement X has lost its "edge", perhaps its adherents should be looking for a sharper utensil"?

Chapter 5 Consumption, Globalization and Multicultural Advertising

Introduction

Western society has entered the post-industrial, late capitalist society since the 1950s, a society characterized by the presumption of consumption (rather than production) in order to ensure the constant reproduction of goods. Consumption is in fact a complicated process of cultural production in that cultural values are employed to promote commodities. And this preoccupation with culture has opened opportunities to multiculturalism due to the need of the expansion of consumption by marketing at various customers (or sectors of market, minority ethnicity especially) since the 1980s. Thus, it is important to understand consumption as it brings about opportunities of cultural transformation, which can be seen specifically in the strategy of marketing: advertising. This chapter mainly concerns the changes in the ad representation with the advent of the culture of consumption. The first part of this chapter introduces Jean Baudrillard's theorization of consumption to show that consumption virtually means consuming the sign value of goods. Moreover, Janice Winship's view of the female body as a site of contradiction illustrates the complexity of meaning production in promotion consumption.

Simultaneously, while consumption is pushed beyond the Western countries to the non-Western countries by the capitalist corporate institutions for market expansion — in the process of globalization, there also witnesses a process of cultural globalization, in which cultural homogenization and cultural differentiation are going together to effect cultural hybridization, bringing about new forms of culture. Therefore, the second part approaches this topic by showing how global advertising is transforming itself through cultural production/representation to meet the need of commodity promotion in the new context.

Part I Consumption and Multicultural Representation

Passage 1

Consumption and the Sign Value of Goods

The essay entitled "Consumer Society" by the French critic Jean Baudrillard (1988) is a useful place to start our reflections on the contemporary role of advertising in the circulation of goods and services. He identifies the new importance of the moment of circulation, and of consumer marketing in particular, as central to the deep-seated transformations in western societies associated with the expansion of consumer culture. For him, the development of modern consumer marketing represents the engine of this consumer revolution-both expanding consumer demand and transforming the very nature of commodities.

Baudrillard (1988) begins his essay by conjuring up an image of a society dominated by an abundance of consumer goods, services and messages and advances two initial observations. Firstly, he suggests — in a formulation which echoes Marx's arguments about commodification and reification — that the new explosion of consumer goods and services products (in his words) "a fundamental mutation of the ecology of the human species" in which individuals' principal relationships have become those with consumer objects and their associated messages rather than with other people. Secondly, Baudrillard argues that in the new profusion of commodities, consumers relate not to the utility of particular consumer objects (such as the capability of a washing machine to wash clothes), but to a new calculus of consumption in which individual consumer objects refer to a wider network of objects and lifestyles. In other words, for Baudrillard, the decision to buy is now based upon the cultural meanings and values associated with particular objects (such as the type or brand of washing-machine) and the consumer lifestyle invoked through these.

For Baudrillard, both these characteristics of consumer society find their fullest expression in the shopping mall. In offering the consumer both a wider range of shops under one roof and by providing a range of other services (such as places to eat and leisure facilities), the mall

> [...] practices and amalgamation of signs where all categories of goods are considered a partial field in the general consumerism of signs. The cultural centre becomes an integral part of the shopping mall. This is not to say that culture is here "prostituted"; that is too simple. It is culturalized. Consequently, the commodity (clothing, food, restaurants, etc.) is also culturalized, since it is transformed into a distinctive and idle substance, a luxury, and an item, amongst others, in the general display of consumables.
>
> (Baudrillard, 1988:32)

For Baudrillard the mall is, in this sense, paradigmatic of a more general process in which everyday life has become totally dominated by the logic of consumerism. The central consequence of this, he argues, is a deep cultural homogeneity. As he puts it:

> Work, leisure, nature and culture, all previously dispersed, separate, and more or less irreducible activities that produced anxiety and complexity in our real life [...] have finally become mixed, massaged, climate-controlled, and domesticated into the simple activity of perpetual shopping. All these activities have finally become desexed into a single hermaphroditic ambience of style.
>
> (Baudrillard, 1988:34)

Having characterized consumer society in this way, Baudrillard attempts to develop his argument further by reflecting on the transformation of material objects brought about by the emergence of consumer society and the system of human needs which he sees as being conditioned by these developments. Drawing upon his assertion about the centrality of the sign-value of commodities to contemporary consumption, Baudrillard suggests that one principal effect of this "play of signs" is to constitute a new dominant form of social communication. As he argues,

> marketing, purchasing, sales, the acquisition of differentiated commodities and object/signs — all of these presently constitute our language, a code in which our entire society communicated and speaks of and to itself.
>
> (Baudrillard, 1988:48)

In addition, Baudrillard argues that it is this logic of signs which now dominates consumption and not the putative needs of consumers. What he means by this is that advertising, packaging and design all work to mark out new desires and pleasures for the consumer which have very little to do with the utility of goods or their ability to satisfy biological needs. He suggests that not only are human needs reconditioned by the system of consumption, but that this system imposes new injunctions on consumers to consume. This compunction or duty to consume is not accidently associated with consumption. For Baudrillard it is central to modern consumption because it is precisely through consumption that capitalist social relations are reproduced. Thus:

> We don't realize how much the current indoctrination into systematic and organized consumption is the equivalent and the extension, in the twentieth century, of the great indoctrination of rural populations into industrial labour, which occurred throughout the nineteenth century. [...] Production and consumption are one and the same grand logical process in the expanded reproduction of the productive forces and of their control.
>
> (Baudrillard, 1988:50)

Baudrillard's argument in his essay, "Consumer Society", represents a very emphatic characterization of contemporary Western societies. What is most noteworthy for us, as I have suggested, is his assertion about the centrality of marketing to the ascendancy of communication in which it is the sign value of commodities which dominates, and in "indoctrinating" consumers into a compulsion to consume, Baudrillard's account privileges the role of marketing in the cultural transformation associated with consumer society.

[...]

(Baudrillard's view of consumption) is a theme even more explicitly developed Andrew Wernick's book *Promotional Culture*. [...]

[...] *Promotional Culture* presents a picture of contemporary western consumer society characterized by cultural homogeneity amidst the apparent diversity of commodity spectacle and consumer choice in terms reminiscent of Baudrillard. For Wernick it is the spread of **promotional culture** which has about this situation.

Thus, while promotion generates what Wernick calls *semiological complexity*, in so doing it also produces a symbolic universe "boringly void of deeper content" and one in which the distinctions between different domains of symbolic production have been flattened. [...] He even reads the consequences of promotional culture in the expansion of a culture of self-promotion. Thus, individuals are tied into promotional culture via the forms of promotionally-based, pubic representations in circulation — from, as Wernick notes, dating and clothes-shopping to attending a job interview.

At the heart of promotional culture are the techniques of promotion associated with modern marketing: specifically, for Wernick, advertising, packaging and design. As you have seen, he argues that these techniques have come to dominate all forms of contemporary communication. Underpinning this spread of the rhetoric of promotion is an intensification of commodity production symptomatic of what he calls "late capitalism". For Wernick this more intensive commodification of social life produces not just more commodities, but a new type of commodity. This is a commodity itself transfigured by the impact upon it of the techniques of advertising, packaging and design which either "transfer cultural associations onto products propagandistically [...] (or) by inscribing them into their actual body" (Wernick, 1991:18). Wernick suggests that this transfiguring of the commodity through the techniques of promotion has significant effects. Firstly, he argues that it blurs the line between an object and its promotion. For Wernick, the consequence of this is to produce objects which are explicitly designed to circulate. In other words, the moment of circulation begins to inform the production of an object. Secondly, and following on from this, "promotional culture" establishes a new relationship between culture and economy. On the other hand, Wernick argues, developments in promotion associated with the circulation of goods become as important to profitability as technical developments in the product. On the other hand, the work of adding cultural values and meanings to products is more firmly drawn into the operation of commodity production. In fact, for Wernick, as you have seen, "through commodity imaging the circulation and production processes have come to overlap".

Wernick's comments, like Baudrillard's, are suggestive in the way they attempt to think through the cultural implications of the increased commodification associated with the expansion of mass consumption and image-driven forms of marketing linked with the broadening of modern consumption's social base. In particular, [...] both writers highlight the insinuation of commercial marketing techniques into a wider field of public representation and the associated "culturalizing" of the objects being promoted. [...]

(Exerpted from *Production of Culture/Cultures of Production*, Edited by Paul du Guy, London: Sage, 1997.)

References

Baudrillard, J. "Consumer Society". in *Selected Writings*, Edited by M. Poster. Cambridge: Polity Press, 1988.

Wernick, A. *Promotional Culture: Advertising, Ideology, and Symbolic Expression*. London: Sage, 1991.

Questions

1. What are the characteristics of Consumer Society?
2. Which is more powerful, mass consumers or objects/goods/commodities?

3. What does "reification" means?
4. How do you understand Baudrillard's view that "consumers relate not to the utility of goods"?
5. According to Baudrillard, what is the result of consumerism? What does it mean by the relationship between consumerism and the "play of signs" that will probably bring about new desires and new pleasures? Can you anticipate for cultures of difference in consumer society?
6. Why does Wernick consider consumer culture as promotional culture? What is promoted?
7. What is the result generated by promotion?
8. What is the role of advertising in marketing?
9. What are the significant effects of "transfiguring of commodity through the techniques of promotion"?

Further Reading

The following part is an extract from William O'Barr's advertising course material "Multiculturalism in the Market Place":

> A growing awareness among marketers of the diversity of American consumers encourages them to pay attention to ethnic, racial, and cultural differences. Multiculturalism has emerged as one of America's most important social agendas in the 21st century. In advertising and marketing, it simply makes good business sense to take the culture of the consumer into account.
>
> Advertisers know that all consumers are not the same in the 21st century marketplace. Special attention is directed to certain "niche" markets because of their size, buying power, and cultural differences. Hispanic (or Latino) and African-American consumers represent the two largest niche markets.

There are others as well, such as Asian Americans, gays and lesbians, and seniors. Many advertisers tailor their messages to the particular interests, market behaviors, and sensitivities of these groups. What is being learned in niche marketing is spilling over into " mainstream " advertising, which increasingly attends to cultural differences among consumers.

Here we know that advertisers/marketers think of and address these important minority groups in American society: African-American women, Asian-American women and gay men. They belong to the groups who used to be represented in stereotypes or absent in ads but are now recognized or present in the contemporary marketplace/advertising.

Please read this part and consider: How does advertising address the issue of the diversity of consumer culture? How are images of African-American women and Asian-American women represented differently now in advertising? Why are gays and lesbians present in ads now? How are these changes in ad representation related to multicultural marketing and consumption?

Passage 2

Sexuality for Sale

Despite its glorifying display of commodities, advertising represents a*moment of suspension* in their production and circulation: production — the sweat and exploitation of work — is over and hidden in its verbal and visual persuasion: the consumption of someone else's (or your own) objectified labour, to which you, the as-yet-passive spectator, are invited, has not begun. Yet in monopoly capitalism advertising has become integral to these circuits of production and circulation: it sustains the moment of commodities, from their social production to their *individual* but socially repeated consumption, which eventually ensures the reproduction not only of the individual but of capital too.

The individual produces an object and, by consuming it, returns to himself, but returns as a productive and self-reproducing individual. Consumption thus appears as a moment of production. ①

By concealing the production process, advertising similarly covers up class distinctions between people, through a form of fetishism: "the definite social relation between men [...] assures here, for them, the fantastic form of a relation between things." ② It replaces them with the distinctions achieved through the consumption of particular goods. As Judith Williamson points out: "Instead of being identified by what they produce, people are made to identify themselves with what they consume". ③

However, in order to identification with consumption, ads move away from capital's terrain proper; we individually consume *outside* the production process:

> in consumption, the product steps outside this social movement [of production and distribution] and becomes a direct object and servant of individual need, and satisfies it in being consumed. ④

In confirmation of consumption outside economics, ads rarely exhort us to *buy* the commodities, but merely to *use* them, hence glossing over the capitalist moment of exchange — the purchase with money. Further,

① Marx, K. *Grundrisse*. London: Penguin, 1973, p. 94.
② Marx, K. *Capital*, Vol. 1 London: Penguin, 1976, p. 165.
③ Williamson, J. *Decoding Advertisements*. London: Boyars, 1978, p. 13.
④ Marx, K. *Grundrisse*. London: Penguin, p. 89.

they never simply sell us the use values of commodities; they sell them as "exchange values"① for qualities in our private relationships with people that are unattainable through the capitalist production process. For example, a commodity cannot "buy" your love (with a man), but ads give just such an illusion of capital's ubiquitous power: "Your face is your fortune: look after it with Outdoor Girl."

Addressing us in our private personae, ads sell us, as women, not just commodities but also our personal relationships in which we are *feminine*: how we are/should be/can be a certain feminine woman, whose attributes in relation to men and the family derive from the use of the commodities. Femininity is recuperated by the capitalist form: the exchange between the commodity and "woman" in the ad establishes her as a commodity too. In ads addressing women this process is insidious: it is the modes of femininity themselves which are achieved through commodities and are *replaced* by commodities. A woman is nothing more than the commodities she wears: the lipstick, the tights, the clothes and so on are "woman". Here are ads not only conceal the labour which produces the commodity; they also, contradictorily, omit the *work* of femininity which women carry out as they use commodities, yet always sell commodities for that purpose. This is in striking contrast to ads

---

① J. Williamson takes the concept of "exchange values" from Marx's use of it as an economic definition: the value of commodities in terms of the embodiment of one identical social substance — human labour — which allows them to be exchanged with each other, irrespective of their use value, their individual bodily forms (Marx, *Capital*, Vol. 1, Ch. 1). But Williamson shifts its use to an ideological level (cf. Mauss's and Lévi-Strauss's "symbolic exchange"). Thus it is uses analogously rather than identically but always retains its relation to the commodity form: "The ad translates these 'thing' statements/use values to us as human statements; they are given a humanly symbolic 'exchange value'" (*Decoding Advertisements*, p. 12).

directed at men, in which the terrain of activity which is appealed to is that of leisure — leisure defined in relation to *completed* work for capital. Women, on the other hand, are sold commodities for their work: the *patriarchal* work of domesticity and child care; the work of beautification and "catching a man". ① This work, like that of social production, is collapsed in the ad into mere commodity (even just to consume the ad itself) is already to have accomplished the tasks of femininity until, at its extreme, it appears almost as if the commodity can replace femininity, can take on femininity without female intervention.

We can conceptualize ads therefore as representing a particular articulation of capitalist production and consumption. But in that articulation they also particularly, if not exclusively, operate through ideological representation of femininity. This *ideological* work relies on, but also construct, an ideology of femininity which is completed through our *collusion* as we read and consume the ads. We are never just spectators who gaze at "images" of women as though they were set apart, differentiated from the "real" us. Within the ads are inscribed the images and subject positions of "mother", "housewife", "sexually attractive woman" and so on, which, as we work to understand the ad, embroil us in the process of signification that we complete. Yet we do not come "naked" to the ads or to any ideological representation and simply

① For more on this work of beautification in women's and girls' magazines, see A. McRobbie, "Working-class girls and the culture of femininity" (unpublished Mathesis, University of Birminham, 1977); J. Winship, "A woman's world: *Woman* — an ideology of femininity", in Women's Studies Group, *Women Take Issue* (CCCS/Hutchinson 1978), and "Woman becomes an 'individual': femininity and consumption in women's magazines 1954—1969", in *Sociological Review* monograph (1979). For more on this work of domesticity, see A. Oakley, *The Sociology of Housework* (Martin Robertson, 1974), and A. Oakley, *Housewife* (Allen Lane, 1974).

take on those representations. We already have both a knowledge of images of women from other discourses and an acquaintance with "real" women in our everyday lives. The signification of an ad only has meaning in relation to this "outside" knowledge of the ideology of femininity. Even when it appears that ads are producing a *new* representation (for example, "Dress to kill"), not merely reproducing an idea of femininity found elsewhere, the signification is not completely autonomous but anchored by the patriarchal and capitalist relations in which we as individuals already have a history and which we already know about.

The signifier "woman" always signifies woman: we recognize ourselves in *any* representation of woman, however "original", because we are always already defined by our gender. Having recognized ourselves in the ad, we are then "freshly" positioned as specific feminine subjects in an identification achieved through a misrecognition of ourselves — the signifier "woman" can never in fact represent us as individual women. It is through this process of misrecognition that ads are effective in producing and re-producing the particular ideological modes in which we live.

The discourse of ad contradictorily places us both in relation to other discourses and, more particularly, in relation to other economic and political positions which, through feminist struggle, begin to challenge patriarchal relations. If we are to sustain and further those material gains, we have also to recognize ideological fields as a terrain for women's struggle. As Coward argues, "the struggle for power within discourse becomes an issue of political importance for the Women's Movement". ①To be able to engage politically at that level we need first to understand the processes of signification which are at work.

In ads, as elsewhere, femininity is contradictorily constructed.

---

① See Coward, R. Sexual Liberation and the Family", *M/F*, 1978,1.

Ideologies of "motherhood", "domesticity", "beauty", "sexuality" and "feminine independence", as they are cut across by an ideology of the "free" individual, are all separately and sometimes jointly mobilized and constructed anew. In this extract, however, I want only to consider some elements of an ideology of sexuality.

To make yourself passively attractive is, by the mid 1960s, to make yourself specifically *sexually* attractive and *available*: as if, it is represented, the act of beautifying yourself is *already* to engage in sexual relations — it is not just the promise of it. This is always implicit: "Girls are coming back warm lipped", say Yardley. "So come out of the cold and into the warm. Be lit up. Alive. All girls." Or "Lips are too sensitive to withstand the sensation of harsh lipstick contact and much too important to expose to experimentation. Super Jewelfast 22 Special is a *new experience itself*. [...] Soft and gentle and kindness itself. [...]" (my emphasis). Or you are perhaps prepared for sex: "Your lips have never looked this wet before"; "You're getting warmer [...] three new bronzed lip-polishes wetter than wet. The warmest colours you ever saw. Each one spiced with excitement."

This ideology of the sexuality in the ad context admits both to a *passive*, virginal and innocent sexuality — waiting for men, typified by the image of a young woman in long white robes and flowing blonde hair ("A Clairol Summer Blonde") — and to an *active* experience of sexuality. However, the active experience of sexuality only takes place in a fetishistic mode (in the Freudian sense of fetish). Women are invited by the ads to respond to themselves through the imagined fetishes of men — the tights/legs, the lipstick/lips which fragments or distortion of them stand for all of their womanness.① Yet since men are absent, there is an ambiguity: is it a sexual experience with men that is inferred,

---

① Freud, S. "Fetishism". In *On Sexuality*. London: Penguin, 1977.

or are women "masturbating" with "phallic substitutes" or through masculine fantasies? "Your lips have never looked this wet before": we see just a woman's red lips, open, a lipstick resting against them, alongside an army of big shiny, erect and partially encased lipsticks.

This ambiguity extends to the more obviously narcissistic representations in which pleasure is self-induced rather than being reliant on men. "Imagine the clinging soft caress of stockings" — a girl, nude, gently holds her ankles almost suggestively, caressing herself and looking out at us (or at men?); or "A touch of Fenjal Silky" (see below). As John Berger discusses and Ros Coward takes up, the naked woman is always a *nude* woman, "framed in the beautiful photograph", a representation comparable with soft-porn photos, potentially to be gazed at by men even if it is women who look at it. ① Thus women not only see themselves as men see them but encouraged in these ads to enjoy their sexuality through the eyes of men. It is a narcissism which, at the moment of self-masturbation and scopophilia (looking, in this instance, at one's *own* body), is also exhibitionist, inviting voyeurism from men. ②

There is a further narcissism which affirms women's self-indulgence and involvement but plays down the sexually exhibitionist elements. "Only drink it if you never bathe before noon. Freezomint Crème de Menthe. Green, cool and slightly wicked." It is an independence of sensual pleasure, however, which we can translate into more heterosexual terms through the visual of the ad: the virginal white of the

---

① See J. Berger, *Ways of Seeing*. London: Penguin, 1972; H. Butcher, R. Coward *et al.*, "Images in the Media", CCCS Stencilled Paper, No. 31, 1974.

② For Freud's discussion, in psychoanalytic terms, of scopophilia and exhibitionism, see "Instincts and their vicissitudes", in *Complete Psychological Works* (Standard Edition), Vol. 14. London: Hogarth, 1915.

woman's dress; the abundant *fertile*, as well as fresh, green of the plants.

This ideology of sexuality is therefore disparate and contradictory for women, though nevertheless contained within patriarchal relations: active/passive; heterosexual/narcissistic; depend on men/independent of men; fetishistic, masturbatory. And it is set firmly even though premised on reproductive sexuality.

The three examples described below have been chosen to illustrate

(a) the construction of an "original" femininity which we did not know about until we read the ad;
(b) its containment within patriarchal relations;
(c) the "penetration" of femininity by masculinity — the "masculinization" of femininity by the commodity form to create a dependence both on men and commodities;
(d) the contradictory modes in which we, as readers, are inescapably ensnared in the signification processes and in those modes of femininity

(Excerpted from Janice Winship's paper: "Sexuality for Sale".)

Questions

1. Can you find any similarities between Baudrillard and Janice Winship's views on consumption and commodities? What are they?
2. What is the "use value" and what is the "exchange value" in relation to advertising images and commodities?
3. What does the signifier woman in advertising represent? How is it related to patriarchal culture?
4. Why does the author think that the image of a woman in advertising is a form ideological control?
5. "The discourse of ad **contradictorily** places us both in relation to other discourses and, more particularly, in relation to **other**

economic and political positions which, through **feminist** struggle, begin to **challenge** patriarchal relations". Pay attention to the highlighted words here. How do we understand the discourse of ad? How do we understand sexy images of women in relation to social changes?

6. "This ideology of sexuality is therefore **disparate and contradictory** for women, though nevertheless **contained** within patriarchal relations". How do we understand the highlighted words, especially the meaning of the word "contained" here? How is the meaning related to multiculturalism and the purpose of promoting consumption?

Part II Globalization, Localization and Advertising

Passage 3

Cultural Globalization

In the media industries — where, of course, we find some of the most dynamic global corporations, driven by basic economic imperatives. In the case of commercial media (film and television, popular music, etc.,) there are certainly aspirations towards creating a unitary worldwide market. Global media corporations, such as Time Warner, Sony and Rupert Murdoch's New Corporations, are thinking in terms of global products and global audiences. This is only possible with certain kinds of programming, however, and for the most part global media interests operate in terms of transnational media spaces (e. g. the "Eurovision" region; the "Asian" region served by Murdoch's Star TV). At the same time we shall see that there are contrary tendencies, towards the proliferation of national and also regional (e. g. Basque,

Gaelic) media. This may be seen in terms of the (re-) assertion of cultural difference and distinction in the face of globalizing tendencies. Again, then, it is the relation between the global and local that is significant: the globalization of the media should be understood in terms of the construction of a complex new map of transnational, national and sub-national cultural spaces.

In one of its aspects, cultural globalization is bringing about convergence and homogenization in world culture. But, at the same time, there are also more cosmopolitan developments, with new cultural encounters across frontiers creating new and productive kinds of cultural fusion and hybridity. In yet another of its aspects, cultural globalization manifests itself as the revalidation of particular cultures and identities (often against the perceived threats of either homogenization or cosmopolitanization), reinforcing diversity. Across the world, there are those who are responding to global upheaval by returning to their "roots", reclaiming what they see as their ethnic and national homelands, or recovering the certainties of religious tradition and fundamentals. Globalization pulls cultures in different, contradictory, and often conflictual, ways. It is about the "de-territorialization" of culture, but it also involves cultural "re-territorialization". It is about the increasing mobility of culture, but also about new cultural fixities.

1. A World of Difference

Finally, I want to go on to look at some broader aspects of globalization in relation to culture and identity. For it is surely clear that the global shift — associated with the creation of world markets, with international communication and media flows, and with international travel — has profound implications for the way we make sense of our lives and of the changing world we live in. For some, the proliferation of shared or common cultural references across the world evokes cosmopolitan ideals. There is the sense that cultural encounters across frontiers can create new and productive kinds of cultural fusion and hybridity. But, where some envisage and enjoy cosmopolitan complexities, others perceive, and often oppose, what they see as cultural homogenization and the erosion of cultural specificity. Globalization is also linked to the revalidation of particular cultures and identities. Globalization is, then, transforming our apprehension of the world in sharply contrasting ways. It is provoking new senses of disorientation and of orientation, giving rise to new experiences of both placeless and placed identity.

One very powerful dimension of global cultural change has been that which has sought to dissolve the frontiers and divisions between different cultures. It has been actively promoted by global corporate interests, — it is an ideal that is particularly sympathetic to those members of the class of symbolic analysts working in the creative areas of media, advertising, and so on. We could consider it in terms of the global culture and philosophy associated with "McDonaldization" or "Coca-colonization". But a particularly good example — because it is so explicit and self-aware about its objectives — is that of Benetton advertising. Through its "United Colours of Benetton" slogan, the company has actively promoted the idea of "global village", associated with global consumer citizenship. What is advocated is the ideal of a new, "universal" identity that transcends old, particularistic attachments. But transcendence is through incorporation, rather than through dissolution. Michael Shapiro describes it as "a globalizing, ecumenical impulse":

> Ever since [Oliviero] Toscanini [the artistic creator of the campaigns] produced the slogan, *The United Colours of Benetton*, the Benetton company has made explicit its desire to

> dominate the mediascape with a symbolism that comprehends nationalities, ethnicities, religions, and even tribal affiliations. The world of geopolitical boundaries — boundaries transversed by Benetton's enterprises — is no impediment to the production of media-carried global symbolism.
>
> (Shapiro, 1994:442)

This global corporate philosophy is further refined in Benetton's most recent campaign, concerned with global threats and disasters:

> In this case, the interpretative work locates the observer in a global community, trying to make sense of the violent clashes of ethno-nationalists. This global self-identification is precisely the difference-effacing stance that Benetton is trying to achieve. The interpretative contemplation of global threats and catastrophes cuts across ethnicities, nationalities, and tribalisms, allowing Benetton to position its products in a universalizing thematic that transcends cultural inhibitions.
>
> (Shapiro, 1994:448)

What the example of Benetton makes clear is the resourcefulness of global advertising, both incorporating and effacing cultural difference in its endeavours to put in place the new global acumen.

A second dimension of cultural globalization that we should consider is that which promotes cultural encounter and interaction. Here, in stark contrast with the first dimension that we have just looked at, we are concerned with the active interpenetration, combination and mixture of cultural elements. These processes are, as Akbar Ahmed makes clear, a consequence of both communication flows and human flows:

> The mixing of images, interlocking of cultures, juxtaposition of different peoples, availability of information are partly explained because populations are mobile as never before. The mobility continues in spite of increasingly rigid immigration controls. Filipino maids in Dubai, Pakistani workers in Bradford, the Japanese buying Hollywood studios, Hong Kong Chinese entrepreneurs acquiring prime property in Vancouver testify to this. The swirling and eddying of humanity mingles ideas, cultures and values as never before in history.
>
> (Ahmed, 1992:26)

Cultures are transformed by the incorporations they make from other cultures in the world. Salman Rushdie (1991: 394) has famously written of "the transformation that comes of new and unexpected combinations of human beings, cultures, ideas, politics, movies, songs"; "*Mélange*, hotchpotch," he declares, "a bit of this and a bit of that is *how newness enters the world*". [...] This process of hybridization is particularly apparent now in developments within popular culture. The sociologist Les Back (1994: 14) describes the Bhangramuffin music of the singer/songwriter Apache Indian as "a meeting place where the languages and rhythems of the Caribbean, North America and India mingle producing a new and vibrant culture". "Artists like Apache Indian are expressing and defining cultural modes that are simultaneously local and global," as Back observes. "The music manifests itself in a connective supplementarity — raga plus bhangra plus England plus India plus Kingston plus Birmingham" (1994:15). Places too can be characterized in terms of hybridity: places of encounter, meeting places, crucibles in which cultural elements are turned into new cultural compounds. Doreen Massey (1993:66) argues for the recognition of "a sense of place which is extraverted, which includes a consciousness of its links with the wider world, which integrates in a positive way the global and the local". A "global sense of place" involves openness to global dynamics and also an acceptance of cultural diversity and the possibilities of cultural encounter within.

The third dimension of cultural globalization that I want to put before you concerns developments that apparently involve a rejection or turning away from the turbulent changes associated with global integration. These developments express themselves in a turn, or return, to what are seen as traditional and more fundamental loyalties. In the recent period, we have become increasingly aware of the resurgence of national, regional, ethnic and territorial attachments. In Eastern Europe, particularly in the former Yugoslavia, we have witnessed the growth of neo-nationalism in its most militant form, but it has also been a feature of Western Europe, with the assertion of Basque, Breton or Scottish identities. It has now become a journalistic commonplace to describe such regionalist or nationalist reassertion in terms of a reversion or regression in tribal loyalties. These loyalties and attachments seem to go against the grain of globalization; they appear to articulate the desire and need for stability and order, as a refuge from the turbulence and upheaval of global transformation. And, of course, there is a great deal of truth in this theory of resistance through roots. But we might, at the same time, also see this as itself an expression of the globalization process — Anthony Smith (1991: 143) writes of the "globalization of nationalism". Resurgent nations are also seeking to position themselves in the new global space.

What I am trying to bring out in all of this is the factor of diversity and difference in the cultural experience of global modernity: new forms of universal culture, new kinds of particularism, new hybrid developments, all of them gaining their significance from their new global context. We should not think of globalization in terms of homogenization, then, in line with what is commonly believed and feared. But nor should we see it just in terms of diversity and differentiation, which is the opposite temptation that many more critical spirits have succumbed to. What globalization in fact brings into existence is a new basis for thinking about the relation between culture convergence and cultural difference.

(Excerpted from *Production of Culture /Cultures of Production*, Edited by Paul Du Gay, London: Sage Publications, 1999.)

References

Ahmed, A. *Postmodernism and Islam*. London: Routledge, 1992.

Back, L. The Sounds of the City. in *Anthropology in Action*, 1994, 1: 11-16.

Massey, D. "Power-geometry and a progressive sense of place". In *Mapping the Future: Local Cultures, Global Change*. Edited by Bird, J. et al. London: Routledge, 1993.

Rushdie, S. *Imaginary Homelands*. London: Granta/Penguin, 1991.

Shapiro, M. Images of planetary danger: Luciano Benetton's ecumenical fantasy. *Alternatives*, 1994, 19: 433-454.

Smith, A. *National Identity*. Harmondsworth: Penguin, 1991.

Questions

1. What causes cultural globalization?
2. In media globalization, is the cultural flow one-dimensional? Why?
3. What are the two consequences of cultural globalization?
4. What does the Benetton's ad illustrate in terms of cultural globalization?
5. Are cultural differences reinforced or erased in cultural globalization?
6. How do you understand in the last paragraph: "What I am trying to

bring out in all of this is the factor of diversity and difference in the cultural experience of global modernity: new forms of universal culture, new kinds of particularism, new hybrid developments, all of them gaining their significance from their new global context?" Is the meaning of this sentence related to "the 'de-territorialization' of culture and cultural 're-territorialization'" mentioned in Paragraph 2?

Passage 4

Global Brands and Global Advertising

The newest challenge facing advertisers was not just coordinating extensive advertising on a national scale, but developing campaigns in a number of foreign markets. In the 1980s global marketers pushed international advertising expenditures to unprecedented levels. In fact, advertising in foreign markets has outpaced the growth in the U. S. market since the mid-1980s. In 1989, for example, foreign advertising expenditures increased 12 percent to \$136 billion while spending in the United States increased only 5% to \$123 billion. The leading advertisers were Unilever, which spent more than \$1 billion in 24 countries; Procter & Gamble, which spent more than \$900 million in 18 countries; and Nestle, which spent about \$600 million in 19 nations. ① Among the agencies Tokyo-based Dentsu Inc. emerged as the leader in worldwide billings, followed by U. S. -based McCann-Erickson Worldwide and J. Walter Thompson Co.

Several factors account for the enormous growth in international advertising during this period, including the increased number of

① "Euro, Pacific Spending Spree: Ad Budgets for '89 Lag in U. S.," in *Advertsing Age* (April 10, 1989), 4, 55. See also "Unilever Triumphs as Top Ad Spender", in *Advertising Age* (December4, 1989), S1.

multinational companies and global brands, improvements in living standards, and innovation in communication and transportation. Multinational corporations with significant operations and marketing activities outside their home country first became a global force in the 1960s. Now companies like Exxon, IBM, Mobil, Citicorp, Gillette, Xerox, and Dow Chemical make more than half of their sales abroad. ① Coca-cola also anticipates the day when foreign sales will account for as much as 75% of its earnings, because there will be many more young people abroad than in aging America. ②

As international ventures became less attractive to U. S. companies in the mid-1970s — due in part to energy crisis, inflation and currency devaluation — foreign multinational corporations began to operate in the American market. Americans began driving more Hondas, Nissans, and Toyotas from Japan and more BMWs, Mercedes, and Volkswagens from Germany. They loaded Konica cameras from Japan with Fujitsu 35mm film and wore more clothes from China Taiwan and Korea. They watched more Sony and Panasonic televisions and listened to more Pioneer and Sanyo stereos from Japan. They drank more beer from Canada, Holland, China, Japan, Germany, Australia, and many other countries.

At the same time, people from other countries smoked more Marlboro, Winston, and Salem cigarettes. They also used more IBM and Texas Instruments computers, sipped more California wines, shopped for food in 7-11 stores, watched more Clint Eastwood movies, and wore Levi's blue jean. And they ate more McDonald's hamburgers and Kentucky Fried Chicken and drank more Coke, Pepsi, and Dr. Pepper.

---

① See "The 100 Largest U. S. Multinationals," in *Forbes* (July 23, 1990), 362.

② See "How Coke Runs a Foreign Empire," in *Business Week* (August 25, 1973), 40-43.

Globalization of marketing became so important that a number of foreign firms made significant investments in U. S. companies. Foreign-based multinational corporations even began manufacturing their products entirely in the United States, such as the Honda Accord in Marysville, Ohio. Other global corporations acquired shares in such major retailers as Fedmart, A&P, F. A. O. Schwartz, and Gimbels. Such investments are made all around the world. In fact, some analysts predict that there will be only a few automobile manufacturers by the end of the century and that the cars they produce will be global brands. The recent operations of Toyotas and Hondas in America may be the first step.

In developing a marketing strategy, advertisers have two basic options: a global strategy or a multinational marketing mix. The global strategy adopts a standardized marketing program with minimal modifications for different localities. For example, Benetton, with its well-known line of Italian knitwear and cosmetics, targets the same customers worldwide — young, affluent shoppers with trendy tastes. The visual images in its ads appeal to consumers in New York, Tokyo, and Paris; the only modification is translation of the copy into different languages. This approach has also worked for Levi's jeans, which have a universal appeal, and for Kodak. Similarly Coca-Cola uses the same TV ads with local languages dubbed in, successfully implementing "one sight, one sound, one sell" around the world. At a cost of $5 million, archrival Pepsi debuted its 2-minute "Make a Wish" commercial featuring pop singer Madonna in 1989. The ad appeared on the top-rated evening show in various countries, airing first in Japan and then following the time zones around the world, and ultimately reaching 250 million viewers.

Most firms, however, found it necessary to customize their approach for each marketplace. With this multinational marketing strategy, each market is assumed to have different cultures and competitive situations.

For example, Tang sold successfully in America as a substitute for orange juice. However, because the French don't drink orange juice for breakfast, admakers repositioned Tang in France as a refreshing drink. In a campaign for Lux soap that appeared in Germany ads showed a celebrity about to enter a shower while ads in the United Kingdom pictured the same woman using the soap in a bathtub. This reflected the fact that Germans are more likely to take a shower while the British prefer to bathe.

Other advertisers used a combination of the multinational and global approaches. For example, when Scot Paper entered the European market, it created a consistently warm, cuddly advertising image in the form of a labrador puppy to tell consumers that their product was soft yet strong. But Scot shot the series of ads in different settings; in Spain the living room had Spanish-style furniture, in Great Britain the setting was a traditional English country garden, and in Italy the living room featured an Italian decor. Likewise, ads of General Motors trucks that ran in Arab countries showed the vehicles at work in the desert.

(Excerpted from Judiann Sivulka: *A Cultural History of American Advertising*, Belmont: Worsworth Publishing Company, 1998.)

Questions

1. What strategies of advertising were used in globalization?
2. How do you understand "a multinational marketing mix" and Coke's strategy of "one sight, one sound, one sell" around the world in relation to culture in advertising?
3. What do you think of "a combination of the multinational and global approaches" in relation to branding and cultural identity?
4. "Coke Spins Same Sell All around the World", in *USA Today* (December 28, 1988), B6.

Passage 5

Global Advertising and Cultural Differences

When global advertisers developed international campaigns, they faced a number of challenges. Among these was the need to understand and appreciate cultural differences. Even the most seemingly innocent uses of colors, numbers, shapes, sizes, symbols, body language, and so on were potentially offensive to a given culture. For example, a firm had to change the models in an advertisement in Thailand from a boy and girl holding hands to two girls doing so because the former approach was considered offensive. And an American shoe manufacturer insulted Southeast Asians by showing bare fcct in its advertisements.

Firms also had to make a special effort to ensure that they were correctly translating the intended message. A poorly chosen name of a bad translation could undermine the credibility of the product. For example, when General Motors introduced the Chevy Nova automobile in South America, it did not sell well — the name meant "It won't go." The Ford Pinto flopped in Brazil — the name meant "small male appendage" in Portuguese slang. Even Coca-Cola suffered translation problem. Translated into Chinese characters, the brand name sounded like "Coca-Cola," but unfortunately the rendering meant "Bite the wav tadpole." Coca-Cola subsequently changed to a set of characters that mean "Happiness in the mouth."

Although American advertisers quickly adapted to global styles of advertising, foreign media proved another challenge. With the explosion of cable television and satellite receivers, viewers could watch channels from around the world. This transformed television from a mass medium to a global medium. But governments controlled most broadcast media, and many did not permit commercials — yet the message somehow managed to spread. Most Europeans now owned televisions, but in less-developed countries only the well-off could afford this luxury, and even then, coverage generally was limited. Lower literacy and education levels in some countries also restricted the use of print media. Among those countries with national newspapers, advertisers typically found the circulation limited to upper-class, well-educated people. To reach this audience, auto manufacturers successfully used TV and magazine advertising, while companies like Coca-Cola and Pepsi successfully reached the low-income market through radio and billboards. Movie advertising, too, could reach urban markets where TV ownership rates were low.

With the spread of multinational corporations and the explosive growth of communications technologies, advertisers faced unprecedented numbers of potential consumers. In this fertile environment the seeds of the nest creative revolutions were sown; the harvest would feature image building sex, and symbolism.

International Mistranslations

Literal translations and mistranslations of English advertising copy into other languages can send the wrong advertising message or no message at all. Here are some classic examples of mistranslations and faulty word choices.

Kentucky Fried Chicken's slogan "finger-lickin' good" translated into Chinese as "eat your finger off".

In Taiwan Pepsi's slogan "Come alive with the Pepsi Generation" read, "People will bring your ancestors back from the dead".

Perdue Chicken's slogan "It takes a tough man to make a tender chicken" appeared on the billboards in Mexico as "It takes a hard man to make a chicken aroused".

Schweppes Tonic Water translated into Italian as "Schweppes Toilet Water".

Braniff promoted its upholstery with "Fly in leather," but in Spanish it reads as "Fly naked".

The Coors slogan "Turn it loose" read in Spanish as "Suffer from diarrhea".

Puffs introduced its tissue product in Germany, only to discover that "puff" in German is slang for "whorehouse."

Clairol introduced the "Mist Stick," a curling iron for hair, in Germany, only to find that "mist" in German is slang for "manure."

(Excerpted from Judiann Sivulka: *A Cultural History of American Advertising*, Belmont: Worsworth Publishing Company, 1998.)

Questions

1. How do you understand mistranslations of the advertising copy or the misunderstanding of the ads intended for a given market ?
2. What strategy would you use if you target at a foreign market?
3. Think of advertising in China. Are all ads from transnational advertising agencies or for transnational brands/products/companies well-accepted by Chinese consumers? What ads are well-accepted?

What are not? Please illustrate with examples the reasons for the popularity of some transnational ads and the consumers' rejection of some other ads in China.

4. In terms of the interpretation/decoding of advertisements, especially in cross-cultural context, what factors influence the interpretation/decoding of advertisements? How would you make use of cultural theories to answer this question? Please refer to Stuart Hall's view on the meaning of cultural text in his paper "Encoding, Decoding".

Chapter 6 Selling Nature

Introduction

Carl Marx points out in *Capital* that capital objectifies and commercializes everything including love and family relationship. In late capitalist age, everything is commercialized and consumed including the human body and "Mother Nature". In fact, while there is the rising concern for the deteriorating environment in the process of industrialization, the environment-friendly consciousness is appropriated and commercialized to promote consumption, as seen in the representation of nature in advertising and the marketing strategy of greenwashing. Thus, consumption is adverse to the preservation of nature.

This chapter represents the ecofeminist endeavour to critique the appropriation of nature in advertising: the celebration of the culture over nature in the pastoral myth, the romanticization of nature, and the employment of the greenwashing strategy to commercialize the thesis of preserving nature. For this purpose, a changing attitude to nature — from the conception of domination of nature in modern, industrial society to the ecofeminist critique of the domination of nature in contemporary era — is introduced first in order to facilitate the understanding of the ecofeminist thinking here. And the purpose of presenting such a subject here is to provoke reflection upon the prevailing consumer culture that is going on now in the globe and to open the possibility of harmonious co-existence with our natural environment.

Part I From Domination to Protection of Nature

Passage 1

Capitalism, Technology and Nature

"Capitalist production [...] disturbs the metabolic interaction between man and the earth. [...] All progress in capitalist agriculture is progress in the art, not only of robbing the worker, but of robbing the soil; all progress in increasing the fertility of the soil for a given time is a progress towards ruining the more long-lasting sources of that fertility. The more a country proceeds from large-scale industry as the background of its development, as in the case of the United States, the more rapid is this process of destruction. Capitalist production, therefore, only develops the techniques and the degree of combination of the social process of production by simultaneously undermining the original sources of all wealth — the soil and the worker."①

Fundamental to my whole approach to capitalism's relationship to nature is that it is, in the end, essentially the same as capital's relationship to wage labour. Without keeping this focus firmly in mind here in this text, one will indeed wonder why I am going on at such length (especially in the quotes from Marx) about capitalist technology's relation to the worker. Capital dominates both, living labour and nature, in order to exploit them both. In both cases, capital uses technology as a mediating factor in order to realize, enforce and reproduce at a higher

① See *Capital*, Vol. 1, Penguin Edition, 1976:638.

level these relations of domination and exploitation. In both cases, the relationships and the processes involved are linked and analogous. Capital is antagonistic toward the natural environment just as it is antagonistic to wage labour. Capital's domination and exploitation of nature, given the latter's finite limits and specificities, leads to destruction, degradation and despoliation of that nature, just as its domination and exploitation of wage labour, given the physical limits and specificities of human beings, leads to destruction, degradation and exhaustion of the working class. Further still, just as the working-class fights back against capital's depredations, so too does nature in ways we are all too familiar with today, such as irreversible climate change, widespread industrial diseases such as cancer, "natural disasters" of all sorts, etc. But in reality, it is not nature taking revenge on humanity. That would be to personify or subjectify nature, to ascribe to it intentionality. In fact, all of these environmental catastrophes, which constitute an expanding environmental crisis, result from capital's technological transformation of natural ecosystems and processes into monstrously destructive forces for humankind which previously, naturally, they were not. Highly developed capitalist domination of humanity and nature has intervened in and transformed the myriad intricate and inter-related natural processes of the planet to such an extent that the current "natural environment" we live within cannot be truly said to be natural; it has been adulterated, contaminated, poisoned and destroyed to such an extent that it is more accurately described as the capitalistically modified "natural" environment.

Capital's relationship with nature has a history of its own; it has a trajectory of development, of "advancement", of "progress". But, we need to ask, an advancement and progression toward what? Capitalism has transformed nature over the years no less than it has transformed labour and the working class. Capital has to such an extreme extent, by today's advanced stage in its historical development, interfered with, appropriated, manipulated, in a word, messed with the earth's overall natural environment that it is in fact increasingly difficult any longer to find any feature, any aspect, any part of it that hasn't been changed in one way or another as a result. This change, this messing with nature by capital has by now done such catastrophic damage to the natural, evolving, inter-connected, highly complex and self-sustaining ecosystems and processes of the planet that the question of sustainability itself in regard to capitalist economic processes in interaction with the natural environment has become an increasingly important concern for the capital class itself (at least at the political level).

The damage to the natural environment by capital can be seen on the smallest of scales. However, it is the overall result of capital's entire ensemble of processes on a global scale that should be the primary concern of communists, of internationalist pro-revolutionaries today. Just as the totality of capitalist production and circulation, operating on the basis of competition is anarchic, because at that level capital operates blindly, driven solely by separate, competitive interests concerned only with value maximization, so too, it seems clear to me, the overall result of capitalist production, circulation and consumption on the natural environment is essentially anarchic and blind; which is to say that, in the context of the transition to real domination, it is inherently and unavoidably destructive and catastrophic for the environment, and, consequently also for humankind.

How did this come to be? One might ask. Since the dawn of its existence, humankind has been subject to the forces of nature. As well as providing humanity with its fruits and various "gifts", many of nature's forces and conditions have served as threats to the survival and welfare of humankind. Technology originates from the need and the will of human beings to protect themselves from these threats and to take greater advantage of nature's offerings. These origins are innocent enough: to meet basic needs of shelter, food, clothing, etc., and to alleviate discomfort and harm. As technics are devised and then gradually developed over time to accomplish these tasks, the technics themselves become increasingly tested in practice, and consequently modified, refined, and made more complex. The technics are thereby improved in their efficiency, at accomplishing the same task quicker or with greater ease, in a word, with less living labour. But the technics are also often made more powerful, capable of greater tasks than were previously possible. As this process of technical development takes place over long periods of time, technical means are developed which are increasingly powerful, which give their possessor power over whatever it is they are capable of being applied to. From early on, some of the most significant of these means were both productive and destructive, capable of being used for either material production or for destruction, whether, e. g. for hunting or killing threatening predator animals or for fighting (or fighting off) another tribe or group of humans, whether in defense or in conquest. Thus, from the earliest times, humankind's technical implements were capable of being applied to the land and natural products of it, to other animals, and of course, to other humans. Somewhere along the way, improvements in technics permitted the production of a surplus-product, freeing up an elite minority from the necessity of onerous labour; then, class societies and civilizations arose with small ruling minorities monopolizing control over the most powerful of these technical means in order to maintain and, whenever possible, increase their class power and protect their accumulating wealth. Technology thus has a long history, in both the economic and political realms, and since the dawn of class-divided societies, its most highly developed forms have been brought into being in the service of a project of maintaining and accumulating class power and wealth. Of course, during all this time most of the technics developed in such societies were concerned with material production, with producing the means of life of the whole society, from raw materials, with technical means, by living labour.

As technology and the scientific knowledge underlying it gradually developed, there eventually arose the idea of humankind's (potential) "conquest" or domination of nature, not just as a dream as it had previously been for a few, but in reality, in a future historically linked to their time. This idea only really became popular with the modern Enlightenment and the concomitant early development of the bourgeoisie. Without going into dates and details, we know that a number of technical inventions in the period of the rise of the bourgeoisie within feudal society gave their masters enormous productive and economic power in comparison with all that had existed hitherto. Increasing domination over nature in the economic realm led to increasing domination over the rest of society, and eventually political supremacy. The process of primitive accumulation undertaken by the ruling bourgeois class dispossessed the bulk of previously semi-independent producers from their means and conditions of production, creating an ever-growing market of "free labourers" renting out their labour-power to capitalists. The latter, as Marx so well documents, began the process of socializing the means of production, by putting together in common work these wage labourers, in a united organized process of production, usually in a single place of work, the workshop. Initially using the same technical means as they had previously as independent producers, the workers were soon to be subjected to technical means and instruments of production, fixed capital, which were owned and directed by the capitalists, and legally protected by the capitalist state. From then on was set in motion an historical process of a constant revolutionizing of the means of production as a result of the expansion of capital and the development of the law of value. Figuring centrally in this project of class domination and accumulation of surplus-value by exploiting living labour in the production process was, and still is, increasingly so in fact, the harnessing and shaping of science to service these aims.

Thus, prior to capitalism, because of the relatively under-developed state of the technological productive forces, with mostly individual producers working independently — even if on a common project under a single master — with their own separate tools and other instruments of production, (a) these producers were still subjects of the labour process and in of control their instruments, and (b) the natural environment was degraded or destroyed by human activity only as a result of either massive over-working by large numbers of producers on a limited natural resource or by reckless deployment of large concentrations of the most powerful means of destruction at the disposal of the then ruling class. Human degradation and destruction of nature did indeed occur, but the scale of it was minute in comparison with today's damage. It was only with capital's historic expansion, permitting its constant revolutionizing of the means of production (and of destruction), bringing about the development of massively powerful machinery and other technical means (chemical processes, forms of combination and organization, etc.) used in large-scale industry that, on the one hand, the direct producers lost their role of subjects in the labour process to these machines (and the science underlying them), and, on the other hand, large-scale destruction and long-term degradation of the natural environment first appeared in history, and began to accumulate.

(From: http://libcom.org/library/capitalism-technology-environment)

Questions

1. In Para. 1, what is Marx's view of the relationship of man and nature in capitalist society?

2. In Paragraphs 1 and 2, what is the position of nature equated to in capitalist society? Does the author agree with Marx?
3. What is used by capital "as a mediating factor in order to realize, enforce and reproduce at a higher level these relations of domination and exploitation"?
4. What is the result of capitalist domination of labour and nature?
5. What does the author think of the history of capitalist development? Is it a history of "advancement" or "progress", according to him?
6. How is technology related to human attitude to nature?
7. What is the result of capitalist appropriation of technology?

Passage 2

Ecofeminism: A General Introduction

Ecological feminism is the umbrella term given to a variety of positions that have roots in different feminist practices and philosophies. These different perspectives reflect not only different feminist perspectives (e. g., liberal, traditional Marxist, radical, socialist, black and Third World), they also reflect different understandings of the nature of and solution to pressing environmental problems. So, it is an open question how many, which, and on what grounds any of the various positions in environmental philosophy that acknowledge feminist concerns or claim to be feminist are properly identified as ecofeminist positions. What one takes to be a genuine ecofeminist position will depend largely on how one conceptualizes both feminism and ecofeminism.

In spite of the so disparate positions of ecofeminism, and the categorization of ecofeminism as a contested point, Karen Warren asserts the important connections between the domination of women and the domination of nature.

1. Woman-nature Connections

There are at least eight sorts of connections that ecofeminists have identified. These alleged connections provide sometimes competing, sometimes mutually complementary or supportive, analyses of the nature of the twin dominations of women and nature. A casual, albeit philosophically uncritical, perusal of these eight alleged connections helps to identify the range and variety of ecofeminist positions on woman-nature connections.

1) *Historical, Typically Causal, Connections.* One alleged connection between women and nature is historical. When historical data are used to generate theories concerning the sources of the dominations of women and nature, it is also causal. So pervasive is the historical-causal theme in ecofeminist writing that Ariel Salleh practically defines ecofeminism in terms of it: "Ecofeminism is a recent development in feminist thought which argues that the current global environmental crisis is a predictable outcome of patriarchal culture" (Salleh, 1988).

Some ecofeminists (e. g., Eisler, 1990) trace these connections to prototypical patterns of domination begun with the invasion of Indo-European societies by nomadic tribes from Eurasia about 4500 B. C. (Lahar, 1991). Riane Eisler describes the time before these invasions as a "matrifocal, matrilineal, peaceful agrarian era." Others (e. g., Ruether, 1974) trace historical connections to patriarchal dualisms and conceptions of rationality in classical Greek philosophy and the rationalist tradition. Still other feminists (e g., Merchant, 1980, this section focus on cultural and scientific changes that occurred more recently — during the scientific revolution of the sixteenth and seventeenth centuries: it was then that an older world order characterized by cooperation between humans and nature was replaced by a reductionist, "mechanistic world view of modern science," which sanctioned the exploitation of nature, unchecked commercial and industrial expansion, and the subordination of women.

2) *Conceptual Connections*. Many authors have argued that, ultimately, historical and causal links between the dominations of women and nature are located in conceptual structures of domination that construct women and nature in male-biased ways. Basically three such conceptual links have been offered.

One account locates a conceptual basis of the twin dominations of women and nature in *value dualisms*, i. e., in disjunctive pairs in which the disjuncts are seen as oppositional (rather than as complementary) and as exclusive (rather than as inclusive), and *value hierarchies*, i. e., perceptions of diversity organized by a spatial Up-Down metaphor, which attributes higher value (status, prestige) to that which is higher ("Up") (Plumwood, 1991; Ruether, 1974). Frequently cited examples of these hierarchically organized value dualisms include reason/emotion, mind/body, culture/nature, human/nature, and man/woman dichotomies. These theorists argue that whatever is historically associated with emotion, body, nature, and women is regarded as inferior to that which is (historically) associated with reason, mind, culture, human (i. e., male) and men.

A second account expands on the first by housing the problematic value dualisms and value hierarchies in larger, oppressive conceptual frameworks — ones that are common to all social "isms of domination" (e. g., sexism, racism, classism, heterosexism as well as "naturism," i. e., the unjustified domination of nonhuman nature (Warren, 1990). A conceptual framework is a socially constructed set of basic beliefs, values, attitudes and assumptions that shapes and reflects how one views oneself and others. It is oppressive when it explains, justifies, and maintains relationships of domination and subordination. An oppressive conceptual framework is *patriarchal* when it explains, justifies, and maintains the subordination of women by men.

Oppressive and patriarchal conceptual frameworks are characterized not only by value dualisms and hierarchies but also by "*power-over*" *conceptions of power* and relationships of domination and a *logic of domination*, i. e., a structure of argumentation that provides the moral premise that superiority justifies subordination. On this view, it is oppressive and patriarchal conceptual frameworks, and the behaviors that they give rise to, that sanction, maintain, and perpetuate the twin dominations of women and nature.

A third account locates a conceptual basis in sex-gender differences, particularly in differentiated personality formation or consciousness. The claim is that female bodily experiences (e. g., of reproduction and childbearing), not female biology *per sc*, situate women differently with respect to nature than men. This sex-gender difference is (allegedly) revealed in a different consciousness in women than men toward nature; lt is rooted conceptually in "paradigms that are uncritically oriented to the dominant western masculine forms of experiencing the world: the analytic, non-related, delightfully called 'objective' or 'scientific' approaches" (Salleh, 1988:130) — just those value dualisms that are claimed to separate and inferiorize what is historically female-gender identified. These sociopsychological factors provide a conceptual link insofar as they are embedded in different conceptualization structures and strategies ("different ways of knowing"), coping strategies and ways of relating to nature for women and men. A goal of ecofeminism then, is to develop gender-sensitive language, theory, and practices that do not further the exploitative experiences and habits of dissociated, male-gender identified culture toward women and nature.

One project of ecofeminism is to expose and dismantle the conceptual structures of domination which have kept various "isms of domination," particularly the dominations of women and nature, in place. [...]

3) *Empirical and Experiential Connections.* Many ecofeminists have focused on uncovering empirical evidence linking women (and children, people of color, the underclass) with environmental destruction. Some point to various health and risk factors borne disproportionately by women children, racial minorities and the poor caused by the presence of low-level radiation, pesticides, toxics, and other pollutants (e. g., Salleh, 1990; Shiva, 1988; Warren, 1991a). Others provide data to show that First World development policies result in policies and practices regarding food, forest, and water, which directly contribute to the inability of women to provide adequately for themselves and their families (e. g., Mies, 1986; Shiva, 1988). Feminist animal rights scholars argue that factory farming, animal experimentation, hunting, and meat eating are tied to patriarchal concepts and practices (e. g. Adams, 1991). Some connect rape and pornography with male-gender identified abuse of both women and nature (e. g. Griffin, 1981). Appeal to such empirical data is intended both to document the very real, felt, lived "experiential" connections between the dominations of women and nature and to motivate the need for joining together feminist critical analysis and environmental concerns.

Sometimes, however, the empirical and experiential connections between women and nature are intended to reveal important cultural and spiritual ties to the earth honored and celebrated by (some) women and indigenous peoples. This suggests that some woman-nature connections are features of important symbol systems.

4) *Symbolic Connections.* Some ecofeminists have explored the symbolic association and devaluation of women and nature that appears in religion, theology, art, and literature. Documenting such connections and making them integral to the project of ecofeminism is often heralded as ecofeminism's most promising contribution to the creation of

liberating, life-affirming, and postpatriarchal worldviews and earth-based spiritualities or theologies. Ecofeminism is then presented as offering alternative spiritual symbols (e. g. Gaia and goddess symbols), spiritualities or theologies, and even utopian societies (e. g. Gearhart). Appreciating such symbolic woman-nature connections involves understanding "the politics of women's spirituality" (Spretnak, 1982).

Some ecofeminist theorists draw on literature, particularly "nature writing", to unpack the nature of the woman-nature linguistic symbolic connections (Bell, 1988). Literary criticism of the sort offered by Patrick Murphy claims that patriarchal conceptions of nature and women have justified "a two-pronged rape and domination of the earth and the women who live on it" (Murphy, 1988: 87), often using this as background for developing an ecofeminist literary theory (Murphy, 1991).

Some theorists focus on language, particularly the symbolic connections between sexist and naturist language, i. e., language that inferiorizes women and nonhuman nature by naturalizing women and feminizing nature. For example, there are concerns about whether sex-gendered language used to describe "Mother Nature" is, in Ynestra King's words, "potentially liberating or simply a rationale for the continued subordination of women" (King, 1981). There are concerns about connections between the languages used to describe women, nature, and nuclear weaponry (Cahn, 1989). Women are often described in animal terms (e. g., as cows, foxes, chicks, serpents, bitches, beavers, old bats, pussycats, cats, bird-brains, hare-brains). Nature is often described in female and sexual terms: nature is raped, mastered, conquered, controlled, mined. Her "secrets" are "penetrated" and her "womb" is put into the services of the "man of science." "Virgin timber" is felled, cut down. "Fertile soil" is tilled and land that lies "fallow" is "barren," useless. The claim is that language that so feminizes nature and naturalizes women describes, reflects, and perpetuates the domination and inferiorization of both by failing to see the extent to which the twin dominations of women and nature (including animals) are, in fact, culturally (and not merely figuratively) analogous. The development of theory and praxis in feminism and environmental philosophy that does not perpetuate such sexist-naturist language and the power over systems of domination they reinforce is, therefore, a goal of ecofeminism.

5) *Epistemological Connections.* The various alleged historical, causal conceptual, empirical, and symbolic woman-nature connections have also motivated the need for new, ecofeminist epistemologies. Typically these emerging epistemologies build on scholarship currently under way in feminist philosophy, which challenges mainstream views of reason, rationality, knowledge, and the nature of the knower. As Val Plumwood suggests in this section, if one mistakenly construes environmental philosophy as only or primarily concerned with ethics, one will neglect "a key aspect of the overall problem, which is concerned with the definition of the human self as separate from nature, the connection between this and the instrumental view of nature, and broader *political* aspects of the critique of instrumentalism" (1991). For Plumwood, ecofeminist epistemologies must critique rationalism in the Western philosophical tradition and develop views of the ethical, knowing self that do not maintain and perpetuate harmful value dualisms and hierarchies, particularly human-nature ones.

6) *Political (Praxis) Connections.* Francoise d'Eaubonne introduced the term "ecofeminisme" in 1974 to bring attention to women's potential for ecological revolution (1974: 213-252). Ecofeminism has always been a grassroots political movement motivated by pressing pragmatic concerns (Lahar, 1991). These range from issues of women's and environmental health, to science, development and

technology, the treatment of animals, and peace, antinuclear, antimilitarist activism. The varieties of ecofeminist perspectives on the environment are properly seen as an attempt to take seriously such grassroots activism and political concerns by developing analyses of domination that explain, clarify, and guide that praxis.

7) *Ethical Connections.* To date, most of the philosophical literature on woman-nature connections has appeared in the area of environmental philosophy known as "environmental ethics." The claim is that the interconnections among the conceptualizations and treatment of women, animals, and (the rest of) nature require a feminist ethical analysis and response. Minimally, the goal of ecofeminist environmental ethics is to develop theories and practices concerning humans and the natural environment that are not male-biased and provide a guide to action in the prefeminist present (Warren, 1990). This may involve developing an ecofeminist ethic of care and appropriate reciprocity (Cheney, 1989; Curtin, 1991), ecofeminist kinship ethics, ecofeminist animal rights positions (Adams, 1991; Slicer, 1991), an ecofeminist social ecology... As Plumwood and Warren claim in their essays in this section, mainstream environmental ethics are inadequate to the extent that they are problematically anthropocentric or hopelessly androcentric.

8) *Theoretical Connections.* The varieties of alleged woman-nature connections discussed above have generated different, sometimes competing, theoretical positions in all areas of feminist and environmental philosophy. Nowhere is this more evident than in the field of environmental ethics. Primarily because of space limitations, the discussion of "theoretical connections" offered here is restricted to environmental ethics.

In many respects, contemporary environmental ethics reflects the range of positions in contemporary philosophical ethics. The latter includes traditional consequentialist (e.g., utilitarian) and nonconsequentialist or deontological (e. g., Kantian, rights-based, virtue-based) positions, as well as challenges to them by nontraditional (e. g., some feminist, existentialist, Marxist, Afrocentric, non-Western) approaches. Such is also the case in environmental ethics. There are consequentialist (e. g., ethical egoist, eco-utilitarian, utilitarian-based animal liberation ethics) and nonconsequentialist (e. g., rights-based animal liberation, stewardship ethics) approaches that extend traditional ethical considerations to include animals and the nonhuman environment. (Some would argue that these are not *bona fide* environmental ethics, since they do not make the natural environment itself deserving of moral consideration.) There also are nontraditional approaches (e. g., holistic Leopoldian land ethics, social ecology, deep ecology, ecological feminism) that raise considerations underplayed or omitted entirely from mainstream philosophical ethics. Feminists who address environmental issues can be found advocating positions within this broad philosophical range.

Where one thinks ecological feminists fit in will depend largely on what one means by "ecological feminism." If ecological feminism is an umbrella term for any feminism that raises feminist concerns about the environment, then presumably ecofeminists can be found along the continuum of feminist-inspired and advocated environmental ethics (or, environmental philosophy). If, however, the term "ecological feminism" is used[...] as the name for a variety of positions expressly committed to exploring woman-nature connections[...]and to developing feminist and environmental philosophies based on these insights, then ecological feminism is best viewed as one of several nontraditional approaches to environmental ethics and philosophy. We are back to where we began: "ecological feminism" is the name of a variety of positions that make visible different sorts of woman-nature connections, claiming that an understanding of these connections is necessary for any adequate feminism, environmentalism, or environmental philosophy.

Whether the connections alleged and the arguments advanced in support of them are accepted on feminist and philosophical grounds is a question the friendly critic must answer.

2. Major Ecofeminists and Their Endeavours: A Brief Introduction

Historian of environmental science Carolyn Merchant published her highly influential book *The Death of Nature: Women, Ecology and the Scientific Revolution* in 1980. In it she argues that prior to the seventeenth century, nature was conceived on an organic model as a benevolent female and a nurturing mother; after the scientific revolution, nature was conceived on a mechanistic model as (mere) machine, inert, dead. On both models, nature was female. Merchant argues that the move from the organic to the mechanistic model permitted the justified exploitation of the (female) earth, by removing the sorts of barriers to such treatment that the metaphor of nature as alive previously prevented; the mechanistic worldview of modern science sanctioned the exploitation of nature, unrestrained commercial expansion, and socioeconomic conditions that perpetuated the subordination of women. *The Death of Nature* wove together scholarly material from politics, art, literature, physics, technology, philosophy and popular culture to show how this mechanistic worldview replaced an older, organic worldview, which provided gendered moral restraints on how one treated nature.

In "Nature, Self, and Gender: Feminism, Environmental Philosophy, and the Critique of Rationalism," Val Plumwood argues that the key to woman-nature connections in the Western world is found in "rationalism", that long-standing philosophical tradition that affirms the human/nature dichotomy and a network of other related dualisms (e. g. masculine/feminine, reason/emotion, spirit/body) and offers an account of the human self as masculine and centered around rationality to the exclusion of its contrasts (especially characteristics regarded as feminine, animal, or natural). Plumwood criticizes both deep ecology and environmental philosophy generally for missing entirely the ecofeminist critique that "anthropocentrism and androcentrism are linked." She claims,

> The failure to observe such connections is the result of an inadequate historical analysis and understanding of the way in which the inferiorization of both women and nature is grounded in rationalism, and the connections of both to the inferiorizing of the body, hierarchical concepts of labor, and disembedded and individualist accounts of the self.

Plumwood concludes that "the effect of ecofeminism is not to absorb or sacrifice the critique of anthropocentrism, but to deepen and enrich it."

In "Working with Nature: Reciprocity or Control?" Ariel Salleh documents empirically women's involvement in the environmental movement and argues that it is a "patriachal belief system" that maintains and justifies both the invisibility of both what women do and the continued destruction of the natural environment. According to Salleh, the rationale of the exploitation of women and of nature "has been uncovered by the ecofeminist analysis of patriarchy." What is needed, she argues, is that "the unconscious connection between women and nature needs to be made conscious, and the hierarchical fallacies of the Great Chain of Being acknowledged, before there can be any real growth toward a sane, humane, ecological future." Feminists, environmentalists, and philosophers must see that struggles for equality of women and ecological sustainability are interlinked.

In "The Power and the Promise of Ecological Feminism," Karen J. Warren, like Plumwood, focuses on the conceptual connections between the dominations of women and nature. She argues that because the conceptual connections are located in an oppressive patriarchal conceptual framework characterized by a logic of domination, first, the logic of traditional feminism requires the expansion of feminism to include ecological feminism, and, second, ecological feminism provides a distinctively feminist environmental ethic. Appealing to the argumentative significance of first-person narrative and emerging ecofeminist ethics of care, kinship, and appropriate reciprocity, Warren concludes that any feminism, environmentalism, or environmental philosophy that fails to recognize important woman-nature connections is simply inadequate.

(From Karen J. Warren's website: "Introduction to Ecofeminism", at: http://www.lilithgallery.com/articles/environmental/Introduction-to-Ecofeminism.html)

References

Adams, C. J. Ecofeminism and the Eating of Animals, *Hypatia*, 1991, 6: 125-145.

Bell, B. C. Cable of Blue Fire: Glimpsing a Group Identity for Humankind, *Studies in the Humanities*, Edited by Patrick Murphy. 1988, 15:90-107.

Cahn, C. "Sex and Death in the Rational World of Defense Intellectuals". In *Exposing Nuclear Phallacies*, Edited by Russell Diana. New York: Pergamon Press, 1989.

Cheney, J. Postmodern Environmental Ethics: Ethics as Bioregional Narrative, *Environmental Ethics*, 1989, 11:117-134.

Curtin, D. Toward an Ecological Ethic of Care, *Hypatia*, 1991. 6:60-74.

d'Eaubonne, F. *Le Feminisme ou la Mort*. Paris: Pierre Horay, 1974.

Eisler, R. "The Gaia Tradition and the Partnership Future". In *Reweaving the World: The Emergence of Ecofeminism*, Edited by Irene

Diamond and Gloria Femen Orenstein. San Francisco: Sierra Club Books, 1990.

Gearhart, S. *The Wanderground: Stories of the Hill Women*. Boston: Alyson Publications, 1979.

Griffin, S. *Pornography and Silence: Culture's Revenge Against Nature*. New York: Harper and Row, 1981.

Griscom, J. L. On Healing the Nature/History Split in Feminist Thought, *Heresies*, Special Issue on Feminism and Ecology, 1981, 4: 4-9.

King, Y. "Healing the Wounds: Feminism, Ecology, and the Nature/Culture Dualism". In *Reweaving the World: The Emergence of Ecofeminism*, Edited by Irene Diamond and Gloria Femen Orenstein. San Francisco: Sierra Club Books, 1990.

Lahar, S. Ecofeminist Theory and Grassroots Politics, *Hypatia*, 1991, 6:28-45.

Merchant, C. "Feminism and Ecology, in Bill Devall and George Sessions". In *Deep Ecology: Living As If Nature Mattered*. Salt Lake City: Peregrine Smith Books, 1985.

—. The Death of Nature: Women, Ecology, and the Scientific Revolution. San Francisco: Harper and Row, 1980.

Mies, M. *Patriarchy and Accumulation on a World Scale*. London: Zed Books Ltd., 1986.

Murphy, P. Ground, Pivot, Motion: Ecofeminist Theory, Dialogics, and Literary Practice, *Hypatia*, 1991, 6:146-161.

—. Introduction: Feminism, Ecology, and the Future of the Humanities, *Studies in the Humanities*, 1988, 15: 85-89.

Plumwood, V. Nature, Self, and Gender: Feminism, Environmental Philosophy and the Critique of Rationalism, *Hypatia*, 1991, 6:3-37.

Ruether, R. R. *New Woman/New Earth: Sexist Ideologies and Human Liberation*. New York: The Seabury Press, 1974.

Salleh, A. K. "Living with Nature: Reciprocity or Control? " In *Ethics of Environment and Development*, Edited by R. and J. Engel. Tucson: University of Arizona Press, 1990.

—. 1988. Epistemology and the Metaphors of Production: An Eco-feminist Reading of Critical Theory, *Studies in the Humanities*, 1988, 15:130-139.

Shiva, V. *Staying Alive: Women, Ecology and Development*. London: Zed Books, 1988.

Slicer, D. Your Daughter or Your Dog? A Feminist Assessment of Animal Research Issues, *Hypatia*, 1991, 6:108-124.

Spretnak, C. Ed. *The Politics of Women's Spirituality*. Garden City, NY: Anchor Press, 1982.

Warren, K. J. 1991a. Taking Empirical Data Seriously: An Ecofeminist Perspective on Woman-Nature Connections, Working Paper, Presented at the North American Society for Social Philosophy. Colorado Springs, Colo.: August 10, 1991.

—. Toward a Feminist Peace Politics, Journal of Peace and Justice Studies, 1991b, 3:87-102.

—. The Power and the Promise of Ecological Feminism, Environmental Ethics, 1990, 12:125-46.

Questions

1. What makes the environment (ecology) a feminist issue?
2. What are some of the alleged connections between the domination of women and the domination of nature?
3. What is blamed as the cause of the domination of women and nature?
4. How and why is the recognition of these connections important to feminism, environmentalism, and environmental philosophy?
5. What is Carolyn Merchant's view on nature as an ecofeminist? Can you find any link between her view and the idea of nature and technology

in Passage 1?

6. Val Plumwood attributes the women-nature link to a cultural origin. According to Plumwood, what causes the women-nature link?
7. How do you understand Plumwood's view that "anthropocentrism and androcentrism are linked"?
8. Why is the consciousness of the women-nature link so important to ecofeminists/ecofeminism?

Part II Advertising and the Commercialization of Nature

Passage 3

The Myth of the Pastoral: Paradise Lost

The Edenic myth evoked in the Princeville ads connects to an equally long-standing impulse in western civilization — the pastoral. Northrop Frye identified the pastoral impulse as one of our cultures' shaping myths, one of our fundamental archetypes. Both biblical and classical in origin, this archetype looks back to Eden or to a Lost Golden Age as the image of the idealized world from which humanity fell. Ever since Adam and Eve (the couple in the ad ?) were cast out of paradise, humankind has been longing to return there. Not being able to do so, we console ourselves with simulacra — representations, approximations — of it. In classical antiquity, the Theocritan-Vergilian pastoral provided the simulacrum in the kingdom of Arcadia, in which male and female shepherds embodied an idealized image of humanity close to, if not actually in, an unfallen state. As literary historian Bruno Snell put it: "The dream of the golden age is as old as man's thinking about the course of the world, no matter whether it springs from a sense of bewilderment, in which case it is remembered as a paradise at the beginning of time, or whether it embodies the ideals of man's positive striving, projected into the end of history" (1960:294-295).

The pastoral myth is founded on an identification of humanity and nature — a harmony and oneness between the natural and the human. In the pastoral world, humanity is in nature and part of nature; there is no division between what humanity constructs and what nature creates. As Frye puts it, the mood of the pastoral is idyllic (1957:46). It is also radically opposed to notions of civilization; as Frye suggests, the pastoral idyll as literary form represents escape from the confines of society, whose artificial norms and structures separate humanity from the freedom of nature. Nature defines the ideal. The development of a highly mechanized and increasingly urbanized civilization enhances the sense of split between the human world in nature and the world of nature, which makes the pastoral impulse stronger as civilization's dark satanic mills extend themselves over the landscape. Freed from, but still rooted in, classical and biblical tropes, the nineteenth-century Romantics attempted to return to the origin of being in Eden or, failing that quest, to seek its image in the unspoiled places of the world or at least to continue to use it as the standard against which civilization is judged.

America has been strongly marked by the pastoral ideal. In its earliest manifestation to European colonizers, the vast continent of America appeared to be a new Eden, a virgin land, where the ripeness of nature provided a bounty for the taking or a field on which a new civilization could be erected free of the sins of European society. Throughout our history, the land, the frontier, the wilderness took on an "immense moral significance," as one recent scholar of the pastoral in American life has put it: "Here was a new continent offering an opportunity, never before equaled, to begin life anew by returning to a simpler rural past" (Machor, 1987: 4). As writers from D. H. Lawrence to Leslie Fieldler have argued, the basic impulse in much of

American culture has been the rejection of "civilization" by an escape to the wilderness, to the rural and remote. The pastoral ideal was enshrined in the early days of the American republic by the Jeffersonian republican ideal of America as a society of rural yeomen living close to the soil. Many 19th-century movements for political and social reform took their impulse from variations of the pastoral ideal — Thoreauvian simplicity, vegetarianism — as did, ironically, the ideology of southern slave society. The quest for the simple life, the life unsullied by the complications of progressives society, remained a powerful yearning, infusing life and art, politics and popular culture, as David Shi has recounted.

1. Advertising, Modernity, the Machine, and the Pastoral

But in the modern age, the quest for the pastoral is complicated by the virtual triumph of the machine civilization that the pastoral opposes. In the age of the machine, it becomes more difficult to find an area untouched by civilization. As Judith Williamson argues in her *tour de force* structuralist analysis of modern advertising, the power of modern, technologically based civilization rests in its ability to define the terms of life so that the constructed world of modern life becomes the norm, becomes "natural." Thus, the terms of the opposition between nature and culture in the pastoral archetype, in which nature is the privileged term, are reversed. Culture becomes nature, and nature becomes subsumed in culture; with this reversal, the pastoral ideal becomes accessible only through the ministrations of culture.

Advertising grew up contemporaneously with the triumph of the machine and the emergence of modernism in the arts. Although often opposed to the depradations of the industrial age and pastoralist in sympathy, the classical modernists' attempt to make over all the arts on a new basis often implicated them in the technologically based culture founded on the power of the machine they feared. "Make It New," Ezra Pound's rallying cry, the prevailing credo of artistic modernism, was also that of Henry Ford and the host anonymous advertising professionals (or those who hoped to turn advertising from a trade into a profession). This credo was their call to a new sense of advertising's role. As Roland Marchand has so ably recounted, with the industrial world poised to offer up a host of new products to a growing consumer population, the world was on the verge of change, and the ad men (they were mostly men) were its heralds, seeing themselves as apostles of modernity. The objects of their appeals, the nascent consumers, needed to be transformed along with the transformation of the economy and industry. Consuming was a novel experience for most people of modest means. But the buying of products suffused with newness was both a prime symbol of transformation and a mark of modernity. The producers of advertising had to develop appeals that would convert a traditional society into one based on new principles.

Marchand perceives several strategies structuring early advertising, what he calls the "Great Parables." Some of these parables (the Parable of the First Impression; the Parable of the Democracy of Goods) tapped into the fears and insecurities of a population ill at ease with its sense of identity in an age of dislocation and transformation, longing for social acceptance and doing the "right thing," which the products, of course, would allow them to do. One of these parables, which Marchand calls the Parable of Civilization Redeemed, works in a contrary way to the others, appropriating the myths and images of traditional culture, especially the pastoral. While most advertising celebrated the superiority of modernity and technology, ads that were structured on the Parable of Civilization Redeemed saw a darker side to the gifts of modern civilization. Along with the benefits of modern technology came a host of modern ills: nervousness, irregularity, physical softness, and ironically the drudgery of the work that made the benefits of modernity possible. The triumph of civilization, the Parable implied, was at the expense of nature. As an ad for Squibb pharmaceuticals maintained, "man outwitted nature — and *lost*!" (Marchand, 223). The overrefinement of food to meet new, modern standards of taste had robbed food of its natural nutrients, an argument used by 19th-century diet reformers like Sylvester Graham, inventor of the Graham cracker (Green). Other advertisers cautioned about the dangers of a body out of synchronization with natural rhythms, the result of the frenetic pace of modern life and the imbalances in diet. The cure for these ills was to reclaim the "natural" in life, something the ads equated with a "healthful, hard-working past" (Marchand, 224). The ads, Marchand writes, "not only contrasted a healthful, hard-working past with an indolent, potentially degenerate present, [they] also seemed, on occasion, to elevate ancient or 'natural' men over civilized moderns" (224). But the ads also reversed their overt message. The cure for modernity's ills lay *not* in a return to the past, but in a further application of modernity in the guise of the products the ads touted. Taking Squibb vitamins or eating bran cereal or chewing Dentyne gum was the answer to civilization's problems; these products restored regularity, provided nutrients, or gave the mouth natural exercise equivalent to an Eskimo's chewing whale blubber. This Parable structure is still resonant in contemporary advertising, as the Princeville Resort ads suggest.

The ads for the Princeville Resort and others evoke paradise in much the way the Parable of Civilization Redeemed did in the twenties and fit into Williamson's category of ads that appear to establish nature, the primitive, the Edenic ground of being, as the standard by which things are to be valued, but in fact evoke more insistently the human-made world. In the Princeville ads, it is the world of "ultra-luxury" hotels, with its concert music, overstuffed furniture, and "the invigorating lifestyle" the resort provides or makes possible, that is the co-equal of nature; in fact, it is culture, or more precisely, the artifacts of a material civilization (golf courses, water sports), that sets the standard of value. This is reinforced by the second ad of the two-page series, which is photographed indoors. Two couples are shown: To the right, a woman is seated gazing out of a floor-to-ceiling picture window with her companion to her left gazing at her; to the left, a man sits at a grand piano while his companion plays a flute. The room is lush with tropical flowers and plush furniture covered in floral fabrics. The colors echo the outdoor scene: purple and yellow. Beyond the window is water and a cliff and the cloud flecked sky. Nature in Kauai, Hawaii, has been taken over by the taming hand of the ITT-Sheraton chain (the builders of Princeville). Wild, untamed nature — evoked in the first ad by towering palms and immense sky — has been domesticated in the second ad, put behind or outside a picture window; the blooms of paradise has been put into pots. ①

(Excerpted from Martin Green's "Some Versions of the Pastoral: Myth in Advertising". In *Advertising and Culture* . Edited by Mary Cross, London: Praeger, 1996.)

References

Frye, N. *Anatomy of Criticism: Four Essays.* Princeton, N. J.: Princeton University Press, 1957.

Green, H. *Fit for America*. Baltimore: Johns Hopkins University Press, 1988.

---

① Ironically nature had the last laugh. A severe hurricane in the summer of 1992 inflicted major damage on the island.

Machor, James L. *Pastoral Cities: Urban Ideals and the Symbolic Landscape of America.* Madison: University of Wisconsin Press, 1987.

Marchand, R. *Advertising the American Dream: Making Way for Modernity* 1920-1940. Berkeley: University of California Press, 1985.

Williamson, J. *Decoding Advertisements: Ideology and Meaning in Advertising*. London: Marion Boyars, 1978.

Questions

1. What does the "pastoral" represent in Western tradition, in Greek and Biblical culture?
2. What does the "pastoral" mean after the industrialization?
3. What does Marchand's "the Parable of Civilization Redeemed" mean? How to cure the ills of civilization according to him?
4. How is nature represented in the ads for the Princeville Resort in relation to the human lifestyle? Do the ads for the Princeville Resort mean new relationship between man and nature? Why?

Passage 4

Media Representation and Cultural Conceptions of Nature

In large measure, the visual constructions of nature in advertising can be linked to, and have been appropriated from, some key conceptions of the environmental movement. The advertisements are effective because they do not contradict the "commonsense" understandings of the natural world shared by many. These compatible portrayals, rooted in ideological assumptions about nature, must be examined and redrawn in order to foster public awareness and citizen action and achieve sustainable social and environmental ecosystems.

Many environmental writers regard the space missions as key cultural markers in our contemporary of conception of nature, the Earth, and the need for conservation: "It is almost commonplace to note how the first pictures of Earth from Space in 1966 made evident the frailty of the planet and sparked a global ecological consciousness." ① Ecofeminist Chaia Heller (1993) writes, "Awareness of the ecological crisis peaked in 1972 when the astronauts first photographed the planet, showing thick furrows of smog scattered over the beautiful green ball." "The planet is dying" became the common cry. Suddenly the planet, personified as Mother Earth, captured national, sentimental attention." ② The mass media presented pictures of the Earth as well as representations of the significant environmental issues of the last 30 years, from protecting endangered species around the globe to preventing the destruction of the rain forests and saving the whales.

Indeed, even though most people have not been to the moon, or the far-away wild places they become concerned with, television creates critical impressions. As DeLuca observes, "in particular PBS documentaries, I learn of and become concerned about the Amazon rainforests." ③ However, television and other media representations are just that, (re-) presentations. They are stories of nature, not the Earth

---

① K. Deluca, "Constituting Nature Anew through Judgment: The Possibilities of Media". In *Earthtalk: Communication Empowerment for Environmental Action*, Ed. by Star A. Muir and Thomas Veenendall. Westport, Conn.: Praeger, 1996, p. 60.

② C. Heller, " For the Love of Nature: Ecology and the Cult of the Romantic". In *Ecofeminism: Women, Animals and Nature*, Ed. by Greta Gaard, Philadelphia: Temple Univ. Press, 1993, p. 219.

③ Deluca, "Constituting Nature".

made real. We know Mother Nature through the stories we tell about her. Our cultural narratives help shape our perceptions. ① Ecosystem, wilderness areas, and wild things are most often unknown to us without the framing of such cultural texts. And those texts will affect not only our perceptions of nature but also the way we act in and upon the natural world.

Heller argues that we tell a particular type of cultural narrative about Mother Nature. This narrative features characters and relationships borrowed from the medieval romanticization of women as depicted in passionate love poetry: "The metaphors and myths of this eco-drama are plagiarized from volumes of romantic literature written about women, now recycled into metaphors used to idealized nature." ② The medieval narrative drama of romantic love plays out in the wistful longings of a man for an idealized, pure woman whom he vows to protect, for his love can never be consummated. Rooted in Platonic dualism, the ideal love is unpolluted by physical contact. She is powerless and in need of protecting. The lover realizes his romantic fantasy only through noble self-control and heroic acts of protection and sexual self-restraint. The beloved deserves because she is pure and chaste.

Heller argues that the imagery of the contemporary ecology movement finds its ideological roots in this cult of the romantic. Mother Nature takes the role of the helpless beloved, and those in the ecology movement vow not to defile her. "In our modern iconography, nature became rendered as a victimized woman, a Madonna-like angel to be idealized, protected, and saved from society's inability to constrain itself." ③

Procter & Gamble's advertising campaigns display similar iconography

---

① Ibid.

② Heller, "Love of Nature".

③ Heller, "Love of Nature".

and the same sentimentalized message. In soft focus, a little girl drinks water from a beautiful indoor sink. In the next picture a deer drinks from a pond in an idealized outdoor setting. The caption reads, "everybody deserves a clean home." This series also includes images of a baby girl playing with a little yellow duck, while fuzzy little yellow duck swim in a placid soft-focus lake in the picture next to her. Helpless and idealized, Mother Nature must be protected from all those who would destroy her.

The sentimentalized renderings of romantic ecology raise many questions. For example, whom does Mother Nature need to be protected from? This category is always vague and sweeping, but the implied formulation if often "human nature," as with Devall and Session's formulation in *Deep Ecology*:

> Excessive human intervention in natural process has led other species to near-extinction. For deep ecologists balance has long been tipped in favor of humans. Now we must shift the balance back to protect the habitat of other species. ①

Condemning all of humanity as equally responsible for environmental degradation ignores oppressive social and economic relations, as well as the unequal distribution and use of natural resources and wealth. Certainly "failing to expose the social hierarchies within the category of human erases the dignity and struggle of those reduced to and degraded along with nature." ② The exploited laborers of the third world who toil in extreme conditions in sweat-shops making commodities for first world consumers are not equivalent to the ravages of global capitalism.

---

① Heller, "Love of Nature". p. 223.

② Heller, "Love of Nature". p. 226.

Overpopulation must certainly be a concern, not only for environmental organizations, but for all of the globe's peoples. Yet some would put the central responsibility for the problem squarely on the shoulders of women — human mothers defiling an idealized Earth Mother. While women own and control only about 1 percent of the Earth's wealth, they account for 80% of human labor power. United Nations population studies demonstrate that in countries where women have become less economically exploited and more educated and socially empowered, the birth rate has declined.

The first world consumes almost four times more of the Earth's resources than its third world counterparts. Those who are victimized by and struggle against the ravages of global capitalism are not to blame for the ecological crisis, corporate practices are. Habitually emphasizing birthrates out of context only facilitates capitalism's ravages of the Earth.

The idea that every person is equally culpable of defiling the Earth conceals the role of corporations in ecological degradation and distracts attention from the production, use, and disposal of resources. Public service announcements and advertising campaigns often suggest that solutions to environmental problems are the private responsibility of individual consumers. "We recycle" and recycling logos on many products are omnipresent, but such campaigns help manufacturing does not make recycling, especially of plastics, more effective, recycling will have little positive impact. The romantic narrative focus on individual responsibility and such socially constructed stories place corporate responsibility outside their discourse.

In this cultural ecodrama that we present, and read ourselves into, how are the characters drawn? What is the nature of this relationship between the beloved Mother Nature, and the protective ecoknight? As Heller points out, the romanticization of nature is "based on the lover's desires, rather than on the identity and desires of the beloved." The role of nature as the beloved is to offer emotional well-being to dedicated environmentalists and consumers alike. Some "daily affirmations" of new-age environmentalism begin to sound very similar to advertising messages. "I hold in my mind a picture of perfection for Mother Earth. I know this perfect picture creates positive energy from my thought, which allows my vision to be manifest in the world." ①

An advertisement for Evian water mirrors these sentiments. Evian's campaign features healthy people delighting in pristine natural settings. On the left half of a two-page ad, a man runs across a blurred, cold, dark-blue background. Across his chest are the words, "In me lives a wildcat who chases the moon and races the wind and who has never measured his life in quarterly earnings." The opposite page is an image of the French Alps, rendered in soft beings tints. The perspective places us on one of the mountains, peering over, but within, the snow-covered, jagged peaks. The caption claims, "In me lives the heart of the French Alps. Pure, natural spring water perfected by nature. Untouched by man, it is perfect for a wildcat." On the left page of the word "wildcat" stands out in boldface, and on the right page "heart" appears in boldface. This graphic design unites the two pages; at a glance the viewer sees wildcat heart.

As with many ecologically posed ads that feature the natural world, this one constructs an alternative sense of place, a pure, untouched environment offered to the ecoknight turned consumer as an escape from the unpleasant realities of modern industrial life. The goodness of Mother Nature is generally depicted in advertising by what she can do for us and most often by the way she can make us feel. Turned into a commodity, nature promises a return to a state of emotional well-being from the strain

① Heller, "Love of Nature". p. 223.

and stress of urban and social life. ①

In addition, the absence of a social presence in the renderings of wild places reinforces a solitary, individual relationship to nature that negates collective action. In the Evian ad, the heart of Mother Nature nurtures the wildcat, the human spirit supernaturally transformed and empowered. This is what Mother Nature can do for us. Such ideas are compatible with a new-age environmentalism based in the romantic tradition. However, once turned into a commodity through advertising, romantic attainment can only be realized through the possession of the product tied to those sentiments. With all those wildcat spirits consuming water sold in plastic bottles, what happens to the environment?

Greenwashing and the Costs of Consumption

According to the U. S. Environmental Protection Agency's (EPA) home pages on the World Wide Web, in 1994 only 4.7% of all plastic was recycled in the United States. Recycling is difficult because of the mix of plastics that cannot be degraded together. Incineration reduces the plastic headed fro the landfill, but it also releases toxic pollutants, including heavy metals, into the air and through the remaining as. These pollutants enter the groundwater and contaminate the water supply. The EPA recommends what is called "sourced reduction" for plastics, to reduce the amount of plastic purchased and thrown away.

Instead of reducing the use of plastic, however, the marketing and distribution of bottled water has led to a dramatic increase in its use. The development of polyethylene terephthalate (PET), the lightweight,

① See Paul Messaris, "Pristine, Damaged, and Nightmare Landscapes: Visual Aesthetics of American Environmentalist Imagery," unpublished paper, presented at the Seventh Annual Visual Communication Conference, Jackson, Wyo. June, 1993.

durable yet malleable plastic, allowed the manufacture and distribution of smaller, individual containers which continue to proliferate. Portable plastic, huge advertising budgets, and profit margin of 40% to 50% (compared to 30% to 35% on soda) have led to an increase in the sales of bottled water by an amazing 144% over the past decade. ①

Thus we have come full circle. The concept Mother Nature helps associate bottled water with purity and inspiration and compels people to express their love for nature by buying individual plastic containers, a substance that degrades the environment, presents hazards to public health, and ultimately has the potential to contaminate our drinking water.

Such uses of mythic nature help cloud judgment, as well as the knowledge and understanding of how consumer culture actually affects the environment. Nature is perfect purity, undefiled, "untouched by man," waiting there, after centuries, just to quench the spiritual thirst of the running man in the Evian ad. As with many advertisements, nature exists to provide solace and satisfy the spiritual longing of those who love her. Like all myths used to reinforce ideologies, this idealization of pure, untouched nature has been drained of any essential meaning. Nature exists only as it is reflected in the needs and desires of the Evian runner.

Loss of any true knowledge of the beloved is another consequence of grounding our love of nature in romantic mythology. "The romantic's

---

① See the cover story by Corby Kummer, "What's in the water?" in *New York Times* Magazine, August 30, 1998: 41. Ironically, "standards set for municipal drinking water supplies are mandatory and are monitored and tested more often than for bottled water," while the bottled water industry has been self-regulated for years (p. 41). In addition, a good portion of the bottled water sold in the United States is simply filtered or deionized.

love depends on his fantasy of his beloved as inherently powerless and good as he defines good."① This type of "knowing" nature is unidimensional and is "wedded to ignorance. Certainly the romantic does not know his lady to be a woman capable of self-determination and resistance."② Just as the true qualities of the beloved are never known to the lover in romantic poetry, when romanticized, nature itself remains a mystery. As long as nature is made myth, is docile and willing to give, she is deserving of love and protection.

However, this is a selfish love indeed. For once Mother Nature challenges the ego, refuses the needs, or engages in self-expression and determination, anything can be done to her. These points are borne out in the most common representations of nature in advertising today, those promoting sport utility vehicles (SUVs).③ While the male would-be drivers are invited to experience the wild world of jungles, forests, deserts, and even underwater ecosystems to gain a sense of inspiration and adventure (again, nature making the hero feel good), nature can also be unruly and anything but docile.

Nature is often depicted acting up, creating bad weather and rough roads. She will burn you, she will freeze you, she will try to blow you away, as one 4×4 ad threatens. This invites the worst kind of treatment, and nature must be tamed. SUVs are most often depicted off-roading; Mother Earth flies out from under the tires that are tearing up wildlands, disturbing wildlife, and breaking down river banks as the 5,000-pound vehicles cleave through them. Domination and mastery over

---

① Heller, "Love of Nature". p. 222.

② Ibid.

③ R. Anderson, "Road to Ruin! The Cultural Mythology of SUVs." In *Critical Studies in Media Communication*, Robin Anderson and Lance Strate, Eds. London: Oxford Univ. Press, 1999.

nature is the result when she steps out of line.

However, simply portraying nature as female is enough to invite a certain behavior. In a Wrangler ad for jeans, a man is given a pink cake by his wife. In the next scene, he shown smashing through the now huge pink cake in the forest, expressing a distinctive adolescent male rebellion.

The romantic gendering of nature has resulted in complicated and contradictory advertising messages that are used for very destructive purposes. Originally, the concept of Mother Nature was borrowed from Native American philosophy and other indigenous cultures. While it may have had a noble purpose, when this concept is lifted from its social and cultural context and reinserted within patriarchal capitalist culture, it is turned into a commodity and commercialized in ways that ironically come to support the economic practices that misappropriate the Earth's resources. This new hybrid of Mother Earth is now a woman destined to be dominated in the same ways that women are subjugated by the legacy of patriarchal capitalist culture.① In such a culture, protective paternalism quickly loses its tolerance when those subjugated — women, minorities, or those outside the dominant social order — express range at their unequal treatment or make demands for self-determination.

This is how we come to such contradictory uses and depictions of nature in consumer culture. For example, studies show that those who purchase SUVs think of themselves as environmentally conscious. They want to enjoy the great outdoors and have adopted a vehicular consumer style that expresses that. At the same time, the ads invite them to

---

① For a discussion of a related position on "cultural essentialism," see Laura Pulido, "Ecological Legitimacy and Cultural Essentialism: Hispano Grazing in the Southwest." In *The Struggle for Ecological Democracy: Environmental Justice Movements in the United States*, Daniel Faber, Ed. New York: Guilford Press, 1998.

dominate nature. Because nature has been portrayed as an unruly female, these two messages are not seen as contradictory.

In addition, a mythicized conception of nature, existing only to please those who admire her, does not invite knowledge and understanding of how humans might best interact with nature. Because of the ways we formulate our love for nature, environmental consciousness can sit comfortably in the cab of an SUV, a machine that uses far more gas than a smaller car. Extracting the greater amounts of fossil fuel needed to run SUVs helps to destroy the wilderness areas and animal habitats, such as the last Alaskan wilderness, so loving depicted in the persuasive ads for these vehicles. SUVs increase greenhouse gases and therefore global warming because of their low emission standards. Because of lobbying by the automobile industry, this situation is not likely to change. The same industry that professes a love of nature fights fuel efficiency, emission standards, and public spending on mass transportation while it continues to make as much as $10,000 gross profit on the biggest and most destructive SUVs. ①This is greenwashing at its worst.

(From Robin Andersen: "Selling 'Mother Earth': Advertising and the Myth of the Natural" in *Environmental Sociology*.)

Questions

1. What is wrong with the present media representation of nature, according to the author?
2. What does the author mean by "Our cultural narratives help shape our perceptions" in Para. 3?
3. What does it mean by romanticizing nature? Is it problematic? What

① See Andersen, 1999.

culture does "romanticizing nature" represent? How is it related to feminism or ecofeminist critique?

4. According to the author or deep ecologies, who destroys nature? Should all human beings equally blame for the destruction of nature? Who should be particularly responsible for it?
5. What is wrong with the representation of nature in the ad for Evian water? And what is the purpose of romanticizing nature (constructing the myth of Mother Nature) as pure in advertising, such as in the Evian ad? How is it related to the profit gaining as illustrated by the selling the bottled water in the U. S. ? How do we call this marketing strategy?
6. What is the suggestion of nature and the destiny of nature, when it is made myth, according to the author?
7. The author mentions that consumers of SUVs are "environmentally conscious". Are they invited to protect or to dominate nature? Is greenwashing contradictory? Is the concept of preserving Mother Nature fictional?
8. Think of the present condition of natural environment. Shall we consume more?

Appendix

1. Victorian Trade Cards and Product Advertising

The late 19th Century saw the rise of product advertising in the United States. One common form of advertising was the Victorian trade card: postcard-sized cardboard ads that were given out at merchant stores and in mailings. Interesting graphics are often depicted on Victorian trade cards and sometimes they have nothing to do with the product being advertised. These cards with product advertising presented a set of values and desires shared by white Americans. So the cards in this period frequently popularized racial stereotypes and caricatures to create the Other status for the minority ethnicity.

(1890s Victorian Trade Card: Alden Fruit Vinegar)

(1890s Victorian Trade Card: Ashepoo Phosphate Company)

(1890s Victorian Trade Card: St. Louis Beef Canning Co.)

(1899 Durkee's Salad Dressing Advertisement, *Harpers Magazine*)

1890s Victorian Trade Card:

Side 1: "Who's dar?"

Side 2: "Golly, I'se a dead nigger".

2. Chicken and Watermelon Stereotypes

Black people are negatively linked to chicken and watermelon. It is possible that they originated in the South or evolved out of American slavery in which arose black resistance through "silent sabotage" — day-to-day acts of resistance, e. g. stealing from the master. And chickens and watermelons are easy for blacks to obtain as they are so common in the southern plantation farm. The linking of Blacks to chicken and watermelon was done in a caricatured manner to dehumanize Blacks and subject them to ridicule. It represents prejudice and discrimination.

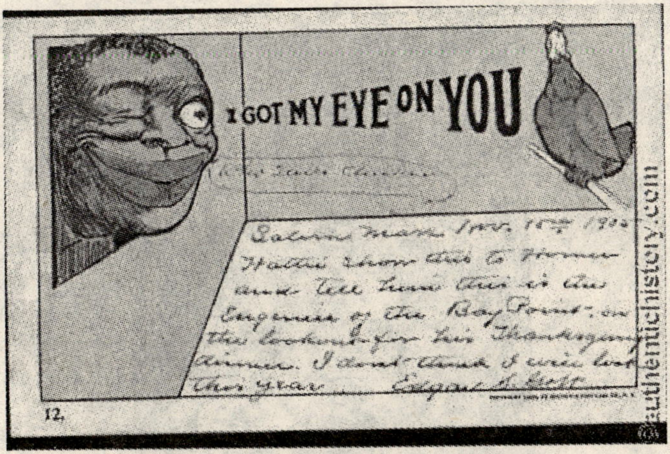

(1905 Postcard: "I got my eye on You".)

(1920s Postcard: Mammy with Watermelon)

"WHO SAID WATERMELON"?
George Washington Watcrmelon Columbus Brown
I'se black as any little coon in town.
At eating melon I can put a pig to shame.
For Watermelon am my middle name.

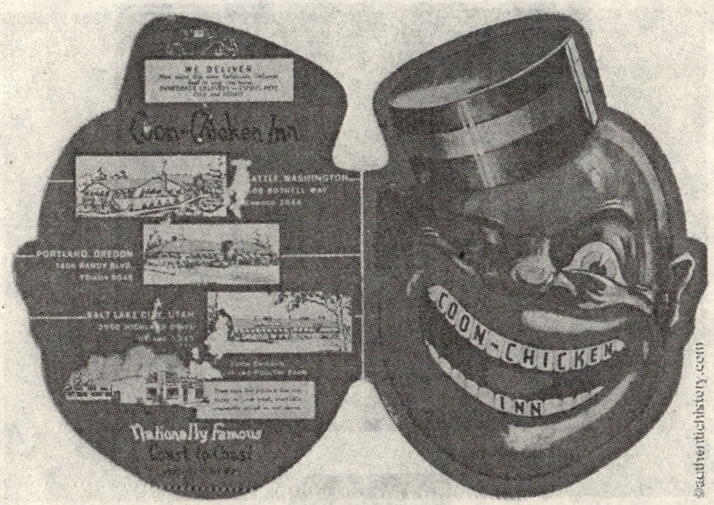

(1950s Coon-Chicken Inn Menue)

A: Artcrafts Showing Stereotypes of Blacks

(1920s Carter's Kongo Permanent Black Ink)

B: Sambo/coon, Mammy and Tom Caricatures

African American caricatures are often found in household items, especially in kitchen items. Most common were the Mammy and Tom caricatures, whose simple, desexualized appearance suggested trustworthiness, domesticity as servants. The derogatory coon items also belong to the mainstream caricatures. These racist household items can still be found in many older American households today.

(Sambo Image)

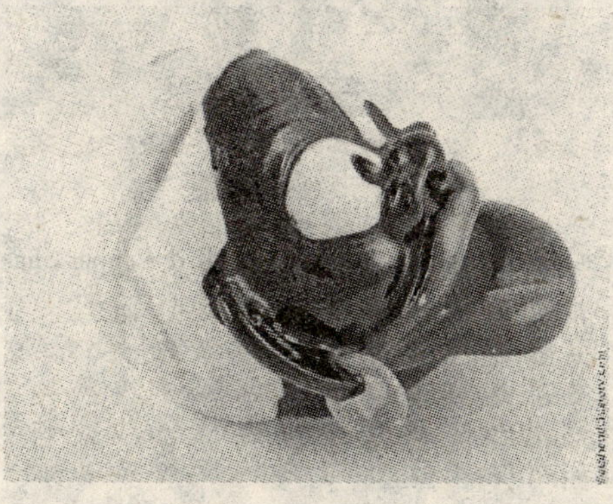

(1960s Coon Ashtray)

(The Derogatory Coon Caricature)

(1950s Plastic Mammy and Tom, Salt & Pepper Shakers)

C: Advertisements to the Present

(1900 Pears' Soap Advertisement)

THE COSMOPOLITAN
CREAM of WHEAT
CREAM OF WHEAT
CREAM OF WHEAT CO., MINNEAPOLIS, MINN.

CREAM OF WHEAT

CREAM

The stereotype of African American children (often naked) as food for alligators has been present since the end of the American Civil War. One is the portrayal of Black people. Imagery of Blacks as "alligator bait" can be found on prints, postcards, and even in product advertising. Some modern-day items still connect Black people to hungry alligators.

(1930s Quaker State Motor Oil Sign)

(1939 Aunt Jemima Ad)

(1937 Ad)

(1952 Van Heusen Shirt Advertisement)

(1930s AC Spark Plugs Ad in *The Saturday Evening Post*)

O'Baby
CHOCOLATE
DAIRY DRINK
"Aint
dat
Sumptin!

OLD
PLANTATION
STEEL
CUT
COFFEE
ROASTED AND PACKED BY
YE OLDEN COFFEE HOUSE
Hulman & Co
TERRE HAUTE, IND U.S.A.
ONE POUND NET

(1940 Ad)

(2000 Budweiser Standup Cardboard Advertisement)

(2002 Ad)

(2002 Ad)

(2002 Ad)

(2002 Ad)